NO AR

W9-DJP-994

Issues in the Digital Age

Online Information and Research

Hal Marcovitz

ReferencePoint Press®

San Diego, CA

© 2012 ReferencePoint Press, Inc.
Printed in the United States

For more information, contact:
ReferencePoint Press, Inc.
PO Box 27779
San Diego, CA 92198
www.ReferencePointPress.com

LIBRARY OF CONGRESS CATALOGING-IN-PUBLICATION DATA

Marcovitz, Hal.
  Online information and research / by Hal Marcovitz.
      p. cm. — (Issues in the digital age)
  Includes bibliographical references and index.
  ISBN-13: 978-1-60152-192-7
  ISBN-10: 1-60152-192-8
  1. Internet—Juvenile literature. 2. Computer network resources—Evaluation—Juvenile literature. 3. Web search engines—Juvenile literature. 4. Internet searching—Juvenile literature. I. Title.
  ZA4201.M353 2012
  025.04'2--dc23
                                                                2011012623

Contents

Introduction

All the World's Information

Nejdra Nance had long harbored doubts about herself—whether she was truly the daughter of the woman who raised her. Ann Pettway, the woman who claimed to be her mother, could be very cruel to the girl—hardly the type of person Nance expected her mother to be. "Her mom was kind of hard on her," says a cousin, Ashley Pettway, who grew up next door. "I used to hear her mom yelling at her."[1] Over the years, Nance's suspicions continued to grow, particularly after she asked her mother to produce her birth certificate. When Ann Pettway could not produce the document, Nance decided to seek the truth on her own.

By now, she was 23 years old and had long since moved out of her mother's home in Bridgeport, Connecticut. Now living in Atlanta, Georgia, Nance started searching for the truth about herself on the Internet. She soon found a database of missing children maintained by the National Center for Missing and Exploited Children. By entering her birth date of August 15, 1987, into the database, Nance found a number of photographs of missing children born on that date. One photo, of an infant named Carlina White, piqued her interest. She could not help but see the similarities in the photo of Carlina and her own baby pictures.

Believing that she was Carlina White, Nance contacted the organization, which in turn contacted White's true parents, Joy White and Carl Tyson. Genetic tests soon confirmed that Nance was, in fact, Carlina

> "For me, as for others, the Net is becoming a universal medium, the conduit for most of the information that flows through my eyes and ears and into my mind."[3]
>
> —Technology author Nicholas Carr.

White and that Joy White and Carl Tyson were her parents. Reunited with his daughter after 23 years, Tyson said, "I hugged her and squeezed her. I just don't believe it. [She's] here in my face."[2]

Wide Applications

If Carlina White had been born in an earlier generation—before the Internet was developed—resources would have been available to her to find her true parents. Chances are, though, that White's search for her parents would have taken months or even years. White would probably have had to travel many miles seeking out dusty records stored in courthouse basements. Perhaps she would have been forced to hire a private detective to help her find the truth. Because of the powers of Internet searching, those lengthy and possibly expensive steps were unnecessary.

With only a few minutes of Internet searching, Carlina White unraveled the 23-year-old mystery of how she came to be separated from her parents as an infant. A 1987 National Center for Missing and Exploited Children poster shows White as an infant and a composite image that shows what she might look as an adult.

Non Family Abduction

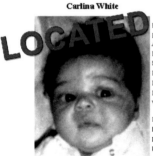

Carlina White

Birth: 7/15/1987
Missing: 8/4/1987
Age Now: 23 yrs
Race: Black
Sex: Female
Hair: Black
Eyes: Brown
Ht: 1'09"
Wt: 8lbs

Missing From:
Harlem
NY
United States

Age Progression by NCMEC 1/9/2007

PHOTO COMPOSITE

The photo on the right is a composite image of Carlina may look like at age 19. She was last seen in a Harlem Hospital room, where she had been taken due to a high fever.

ANYONE HAVING INFORMATION SHOULD CONTACT
The National Center for Missing and Exploited Children
1-800-843-5678 (1-800-THE-LOST) OR
New York City Police Department (New York) 1-212-694-7781
Or Your Local FBI

The case illustrates how a simple Internet search that took no more than a few minutes was instrumental in solving a mystery that had endured for nearly a quarter of a century. Most Internet searches produce far less dramatic results—they are used by students to research school assignments, by journalists and authors looking for facts for their stories and books, and by doctors, scientists, and other professional people who are constantly tapping databases in search of information needed to do their jobs. "For me, as for others, the Net is becoming a universal medium, the conduit for most of the information that flows through my eyes and ears and into my mind," says Nicholas Carr, an author who has written several books on technology. "The advantages of having immediate access to such an incredibly rich store of information are many, and they've been widely described and duly applauded."[3]

But the information found on the Internet has wider applications that touch the lives of virtually all Americans as well as tens of millions of people in other countries. Shoppers trawl through the Internet to compare prices and seek the best deals. Singles join Internet-based dating services to help match them with compatible partners. Fantasy football league players search

> "Nearly any question one might frame can be answered in one way or another by mining the [database] that is building second by second across the Internet."[4]
>
> — John Battelle, former editor of *Wired* magazine.

the Internet for news about their players as they seek to gain advantages over their rivals. Participants in social networking sites such as Facebook use the information they find on the Internet to discover long lost friends. The list of applications for Internet information grows with each question that an Internet user needs answered. Commenting on how searching for information on the Internet has become an international pastime, former *Wired* magazine editor John Battelle says,

> What do Japanese teenagers think is cool this week? What pop star is selling, and who is falling off the charts? Which politician is popular in Iowa, New Hampshire, or California, and why? Where do suburban moms get their answers about cancer? Who visits terrorist-related or pornography sites, and how do visitors find them? What type of insurance do Latino men buy, and why?

How do university students in China get their news? Nearly any question one might frame can be answered in one way or another by mining the [database] that is building second by second across the Internet.[4]

Imagining Life Without the Internet

Given the wide range of information found online, what life would be like without the Internet may be difficult for many people to imagine. Without access to online critiques by customers, out-of-town visitors searching for places to eat would have to take their chances at unfamiliar restaurants. Without access to online auction sites, collectors hoping to buy vintage baseball cards would have to spend a lot of their free time visiting trade shows. Without access to online databases, students and other researchers would have to spend many hours poring through periodicals searching for articles they need to complete their assignments. And without access to an online database of missing children, chances are Carlina White might still be searching for her true parents.

Chapter One

Evolution of the Information Superhighway

In Hackensack, New Jersey, Pascack Regional High School has launched a program to ensure every student has access to a laptop computer. For 16-year-old Pascack student Josh Walker, his laptop has become his constant companion—it is always at hand so that he can access his class assignments, notes and, especially, Google. "You can Google basically anything,"[5] says Walker, who has found the online search engine to be as important to his schoolwork as his pens and notebooks.

However, to Walker and millions of other young people, Google is much more than a study aid. The search engine is always available to answer questions not only about schoolwork but also about movies they want to see, sports teams they enjoy following, and video games they think about buying. Essentially, anytime Walker needs a question answered, he turns first to Google. "That's also one of the disadvantages," he quickly adds. "It could distract you from doing your homework."[6]

The Most Popular Search Engine

Walker's comments illustrate how Google and similar search engines have grown to dominate the Internet. Google is only one search engine, to be sure, but it is the most popular search engine used in America and other parts of the world as well. Indeed, some 68 percent of Internet searches—worldwide, about 2.4 billion a day—are performed using Google. "Google has become the front door to the world for many people, the place they go for information," says Michael Moritz, a financial adviser who specializes in technology companies. "It is probably the most visible service concocted by mankind."[7]

Google is so ubiquitous that it has entered the English language as more than a proper noun. In 2006 the *Merriam-Webster* dictionary declared "google" a verb. To "google," according to the dictionary, is to use the Google search engine to seek information on the Internet about a person, place, or thing. "A noun turns into a verb very often," says Thomas Pitoniak, the associate editor for Merriam-Webster. "Because they have achieved so much prominence in the world of search, people have been using the word Google as a generic verb now. Our main aim is to respond to the use of the language that we see."[8]

There are, of course, other search engines. Trailing behind Google, in a distant second place, is Bing, which was established by software giant Microsoft to compete with Google. By 2011 Bing was being used to perform 27 percent of all Internet searches—well below the number of searches that employ Google.

The world's most popular search engine, Google, is used for information searches of all kinds. Worldwide, Google performs approximately 2.4 billion searches a day.

The First Online Community

In addition to Google and Bing there are dozens of other search engines. Some, like Google and Bing, are intended for general-purpose searching, but others are highly specialized. Some require paid subscriptions. Some look for photos, videos, job openings, medical information, news alerts, and even singles seeking dates. Investors can use financial-oriented search engines to find stock prices and backgrounds and histories of companies as well as predictions by experts on whether those companies may be good investments.

Most online retail sites have their own search engines, enabling shoppers to find the products they seek by entering keywords, price, or other criteria. Shoppers using the familiar Amazon.com website to search for books (or thousands of other products) can find not only the books they desire but also summaries of the contents, options to buy various editions—both used and new—and the sales ranks of the books: in other words, their popularity among other Amazon shoppers. Many of the books listed on the Amazon.com site have also been digitized, giving prospective buyers a sneak peek inside.

> "Google has become the front door to the world for many people, the place they go for information. It is probably the most visible service concocted by mankind."[7]
>
> — Michael Moritz, a financial adviser who specializes in technology companies.

Amazon.com was founded in 1994 as predominantly an online seller of books, although today the retailer sells all manner of consumer products. Prior to the establishment of Amazon.com and similar retailers, anybody who wanted to buy a book either had to go to a bookstore or do business with a mail-order retailer. Finding a book to buy usually meant either going to the bookstore and browsing through the inventory on the shelves or paging through a catalog sent to the customer's home by the mail-order seller. Certainly, the information a customer needed to make a selection was available; however, it may have taken considerable time, and inconvenience, before the customer found the book he or she was seeking.

For online shoppers, though, Amazon.com and similar retailers could expedite the search process. By using the company's search engine, customers could find information on the books they desire in a matter

How Much Information Is on the Internet?

Typically, websites include more than a single page of data. Most include multiple pages, each with its own address or uniform resource locator (URL). Google started counting URLs in 1998. That year, the search engine announced the existence of 26 million unique URLs on the Internet. In 2000 the number of URLs passed the 1 billion mark. In 2008 Google announced that the number of URLs found on the Internet numbered more than 1 trillion.

Google software engineers Jesse Alpert and Nissan Hajaj speculated that the Internet could be even larger. They pointed out that the statistic of 1 trillion URLs does not, for example, include web-based calendars that automatically add more links every day. In addition, Google has also found that many web pages are exact duplicates of themselves, and has not counted the duplicates in the total. "So how many unique pages does the web really contain?" asked Alpert and Hajaj in a Google blog. "We don't know; we don't have time to look at them all."

Jesse Alpert and Nissan Hajaj, "We Knew the Web Was Big . . . ," Official Google Blog, July 25, 2008. http://googleblog.blogspot.com.

of seconds—eliminating the need to drive to the mall or fill out an order form that would have to be mailed, perhaps cross-country, to the mail-order bookseller.

Moreover, Amazon.com has offered another dimension to the shopping experience. The company has given readers the opportunity to comment on the books listed for sale. It means consumers have much more information than had been previously available to them when they bought their books from brick-and-mortar retailers or through catalogs. People like themselves help customers make the selections. "Amazon was probably the first truly worldwide community that was built online," says Scott Lipsky, a former Amazon.com executive. "They happened to sell books. But the simple fact that everyone was sharing their thoughts and book reviews made it a community unto itself."[9]

Birth of the Internet

Of course, Amazon.com and similar retailers could not have been launched without the Internet. In fact, when Amazon.com was launched the Internet was already 25 years old, but for much of that period its potential as a deliverer of information was largely untapped.

Officially, the Internet was born on October 29, 1969. At 10:30 p.m. that evening, a computer at the University of California at Los Angeles communicated with a computer at Stanford University in Palo Alto, California—a distance of some 300 miles. The message traveled over telephone lines. The first word to be transmitted over the Internet was "lo." The message was supposed to have read "log in," but the computer crashed before the whole message was sent. The engineers rebooted and tried again, managing to transmit the message in full on their second attempt.

> "The more information there is out there, the more likely you are to get junk or lies for an answer. You want relevant information, but you are fighting with chaos." [13]
>
> — Google cofounder Larry Page.

The project was underwritten by a US Defense Department agency, Advanced Research Projects Agency Network (ARPANET), which was seeking a way for the different branches of the military to share the information they had stored on computers in the event a war wiped out normal communications. Within a few years, the military gave access to what became known as the Internet to universities, private businesses, and individuals.

The First Web Browsers

By the late 1980s an abundant amount of technical information was stored online, but finding it often posed a challenge. "Academics and technologists were regularly using the Internet to store papers, technical specs and other kinds of documents on machines that were publicly accessible," says John Battelle. "Unless you had the exact machine address and file name, however, it was nearly impossible to find those archives." [10]

Throughout this period, Internet users accessed data over what was known as Usenet—essentially an online bulletin board that was created in

1979 by Duke University graduate students Jim Ellis and Tom Truscott. Information appeared in text form in what were known as "newsgroups." Anybody could post data in a newsgroup. Many newsgroups covered technical data, but many also covered areas of interest in sports, popular culture, political issues, and hundreds of other topics.

The portion of the Internet known as the World Wide Web arrived in 1991 when Swiss engineer Tim Berners-Lee combined a number of software tools, enabling designers to create web pages featuring text and graphics. A major breakthrough in the development of the web was achieved when Berners-Lee provided links that enabled users to jump from one page to another. This was the birth of the Internet address—the URL, or uniform resource identifier. To enable travel from URL to URL, software known as web browsers were developed. The first browser to be developed was Mosaic; it was eventually replaced by Internet Explorer, Firefox, and others.

The First Search Engine

Meanwhile, Alan Emtage, a computer-engineering student at McGill University in Montreal, Canada, developed the first search engine, which he named Archie. Originally the program was named Archives, but it was shortened to Archie, named after Archie Andrews, the perennial comic book teenager. To search the Internet with Archie, the user entered keywords into the search bar. Archie responded by creating a directory of sites that included those keywords. Users could then retype the Internet addresses in order to connect to the sites and trawl through the data. A later version, named Veronica by its creators, improved on Archie's performance, making more of the Internet available through search. Another early search engine, Jughead, enabled the user to follow links to sites indexed by the search. (Comic book readers recognized the names of Veronica and Jughead as Archie's friends.)

> "Searching the Internet is one of the earliest activities people try when they first start using the Internet, and most users quickly feel comfortable with the act of searching. Users paint a very rosy picture of their online search experiences." [15]
>
> — Pew Internet & American Life Project.

All that these early versions of search engines indexed were titles. Therefore, if a searcher did not enter keywords that were contained in the document's title, Archie and the other early search engines would fail to produce the document.

The AltaVista Revolution

Although the capabilities of Archie, Veronica, and Jughead were limited, in reality there was not much available on the Internet that anybody other than software engineers and others involved in high-tech research cared to read. During this era little consumer-oriented information was available on the Internet. Indeed, in 1993 just 130 nontechnical websites were in existence.

That would soon change. Within three years the Internet contained more than 600,000 websites. Now the need was for a computer program that could sift through the thousands of pages of information on the web, providing the user with data that he or she requested. At Digital Equipment Company (DEC), one of the first manufacturers of computer hardware, engineers produced the first search engine designed to perform keyword scans across the Internet.

It was named AltaVista, and it was released free to the public on December 15, 1995. On its first day of availability, some 300,000 computer users employed the program to conduct Internet searches. In its first year of availability, AltaVista performed 4 billion searches.

A search engine requires three components to search the web. The first is a function that acts as a spider, crawling along every available website on the Internet, collecting the information the user desires. The second component is the ability to create an index based on the keywords entered by the user. The third component is the interface—the ability to present the information in a format the user understands. AltaVista was the first search engine to incorporate all three components.

The Wisdom of Crowds

As searching became a bigger part of Internet use, dozens of new search engines became available. Among them were Excite, LookSmart, Yahoo,

A seemingly infinite number of books, CDs, and other media fill the Amazon.com warehouse (pictured). Consumers are increasingly turning to online retail sites such as this one because they expedite and simplify the search for all sorts of items.

WebCrawler, and Infoseek. All worked in basically the same way: They used spiders to crawl along the World Wide Web, collecting and indexing sites based on the number of views they were receiving. In other words, the most visited websites would be listed at the top of the so-called organic results produced by the search engine.

The World Wide Web

The Internet is often referred to as the World Wide Web. The web is found on the Internet, but the Internet was in existence before the launch of the web.

Throughout the 1970s and 1980s, most information on the Internet was found in text form. Early Internet service providers, such as AOL (then known as America Online), sought to spruce up the information by introducing color and graphics. To achieve this goal, Internet service providers developed software known as graphic user interfaces (GUIs). For much of this era, the GUIs were only modestly successful—the information appeared on most users' screens as long columns of text.

In the meantime, software engineers developed hypertexting—enabling the user to jump to a new screen of information after clicking on a word in text. With the development of the uniform resource locator, or URL, every page of information could be assigned a unique Internet address. In 1991 Swiss engineer Tim Berners-Lee combined all these factors—hypertexting, assignment of unique URL addresses, and improved color and graphics—to create the first web pages. The arrival of AltaVista and other search engines soon followed, providing users with tools to search pages on the World Wide Web.

These search engines served as tremendous aids to Internet users, but their chief strength—indexing websites according to keywords—also turned out to be their chief weakness. AltaVista and the other search engines developed their indexes based on the number of anonymous hits the sites received. They could not judge the quality of the information they produced—only that a lot of other people had used the same keywords to find them. "If you did a search for *university* on AltaVista, it heaved at you every text that contained the word *university*, without ranking value or assessing whether people were actually using the links,"[11] says technology writer Ken Auletta.

In 1996 two graduate students at Stanford University, Larry Page and Sergey Brin, found a new way to index information. They developed an algorithm—the mathematical formula that drives the software—that assesses the number of links other websites have established for the pages. They named the system "PageRank."

Brin and Page reasoned that these links represented endorsements by other website administrators, giving those pages a measure of credibility—a factor that is far more important to searchers than websites that simply receive a high number of anonymous hits. Therefore, the search engine developed by Page and Brin created an index that ranked the organic results on the strength of how many other links were leading Internet users to the sites. Page and Brin would use the algorithm to concoct a new search engine which they named Google. Says Internet marketing consultant Aaron Goldman, "In other words, Google taps the wisdom of crowds to help determine what no computer can—just how good is that content?"[12]

Part of American Life

At first, Page and Brin named their search engine BackRub but later changed it to Google—a play on the word *googol*, which is a number represented by 1 followed by 100 zeroes. Page and Brin selected the name because it reflected their desire to organize an enormous amount of information. "The more information there is out there, the more likely you are to get junk or lies for an answer," says Page. "You want relevant information, but you are fighting with chaos."[13]

> "I do think there are people out there who are dying because they're getting too much information and they don't know how to handle it."[17]
>
> — Psychologist David Lewis.

In addition to ranking web pages according to the number of links they receive, PageRank is also able to assess the importance of some links, giving more weight to links that are regarded as authorities on the issue that is the subject of the search. "Before this, people were just looking at the content," says Rajeev Motwani, associate professor of computer science at Stanford University. "They were completely ignoring the fact that people were going to the effort of putting a link from one page to another and there must be meaning to that."[14]

Google soon proved to be enormously successful, drawing users by the tens of millions—and making ordinary Americans into

Internet searchers. In fact, in the typical American home, searching the Internet became a common part of life. According to a 2008 report by the Pew Internet & American Life Project, in 2002 searching the Internet was a daily occurrence in just 22 percent of American homes; by 2008 searching the Internet had expanded, representing a daily occurrence in 49 percent of American homes. Said a related 2005 Pew study:

> Searching the Internet is one of the earliest activities people try when they first start using the Internet, and most users quickly feel comfortable with the act of searching. Users paint a very rosy picture of their online search experiences. They feel in control as searchers: nearly all express confidence in their searching skills. They are happy with the results they find; again, nearly all report that they are usually successful in finding what they are looking for.[15]

The 2008 Pew study cited a number of reasons for the increase in use of search engines, one of which was the wider availability of high-speed Internet connections. Clearly, though, the Pew study points out that search engines have become a much more vital part of Internet use because of the explosive growth of the Internet. With millions of websites, blogs, news sites, image archives, and video archives, the Internet has become a very cluttered place.

The Pew study suggests that people find the use of search engines to be a very convenient and inexpensive tool in helping them cut through the clutter. Says the Pew report,

> Users can now expect to find a high-performing, site-specific search engine on just about every content-rich website that is worth its salt. With a growing mass of Web content from blogs, news sites, image and video archives, personal websites and more, Internet users have an option to turn not only to the major search engines, but also to search engines on individual sites, as vehicles to reach the information they are looking for.[16]

Information Overload

Despite the reliance on search engines by Internet users, some critics believe search engines contribute to information overload—a circumstance in which so much information is available that people can find themselves drowning (virtually) in the flood of data that appears on their screens. Indeed, medical studies have actually indicated that when searches performed through Google and other search engines produce too many results, people manifest physical reactions. These reactions include indigestion and a rise in blood pressure. "On the physical level, you might find people having digestive problems. They may, if the stress is chronic, have problems with their heart—hypertension, high blood pressure," says psychologist David Lewis, who has studied the effects of information overload. "No matter how interesting your job is, it's probably not worth dying for. I do think there are people out there who are dying because they're getting too much information and they don't know how to handle it."[17]

Information overload may not have been an unexpected development. In its earliest days, the Internet was referred to as the "information superhighway," a term often attributed to former vice president Al Gore, one of the Internet's earliest and most enthusiastic boosters. To many Internet users, the amount of information barreling down the information superhighway was overwhelming. Search engines were helpful in organizing the data, yet the amount of data still seemed too voluminous to pick through.

After entering keywords, the typical Google searcher will find hundreds of thousands of pages at his or her fingertips—when all that he or she really desires to see is perhaps a dozen or so. Critics wonder why search engines like Google even bother offering so many options based on a few simple keywords. "It takes only one or two pages of Google hits to overwhelm the average reader," says Harvard University history professor Ann Blair. "Does it really matter whether there are hundreds of thousands more pages after those?"[18]

Teaching Search

Moreover, other critics wonder whether Google and the other search engines—even with their technical sophistication—can keep up with the vast amount of information available on the Internet. Says Andrew Kantor, the former editor of *PC Magazine,* "The amount of stuff on the Internet is of a magnitude larger than any previous collection of any sort. We're reaching the point where it's too large to be effectively searched, filed, indexed, briefed, organized, or numbered."[19] In a little more than 20 years, the Internet has grown from just a handful of websites to an estimate of nearly 130 million. "'Unwieldy' doesn't begin to describe it,"[20] Kantor says.

Kantor says that for many years, casual Internet users could usually find what they needed by entering a few general search terms. Now, though, he says searching has turned into something of a science. For Internet users to find what they need in search engine results, Kantor says they require a degree of sophistication in knowing how to hone their searches. He says, "Unless you narrow your search down with a long list of carefully chosen search terms, you'll end up with hundreds, thousands, or even millions of results."[21]

Given the growing complexity of the Internet and the volumes of information now available, many experts advocate that search training should become an integral part of teaching computer skills to young people and others. Says Greg R. Notess, reference librarian at Montana State University,

> If, as some would have us believe, people can just go to Google, enter a couple of words, click the search button, and magically get all the information they could possibly want, what remains to be taught?

> The answer lies behind the seeming ease and speed of today's search engines. The colossal amount of information freely available on the Web is sometimes easy to find and at other times manages to hide from all but the most skilled searchers. But the truth is, the success of your quest depends completely on the kind of information you need and how important the right answer is. In fact, Web search engines, even Google, are still a long way from providing access to all information. They do not begin to search all the information available on the Internet.[22]

In 1996, Larry Page (left) and Sergey Brin (right) found a new way to index online information. Their idea for increasing the amount of relevant information obtained through online searching formed the basis of the search engine now known as Google.

New Challenges Ahead

Given the enormous amount of information available at the fingertips of Internet users, many schools and universities have found ways to provide instruction to students in the skills they need to perform effective Internet searches. Says Notess, "Most users don't understand how complex the search process can be and they may not grasp the complexity of the search engine systems, but they seem to be aware of inconsistencies in search engine results. They know search engines keep changing, and they recognize they have more to learn about the search process."[23]

At many schools, the chore of educating young people in the proper way to search the Internet has fallen on librarians. Some, like Indiana University librarian Jeff Humphrey, schedule seminars that vary in length from an hour to day-long sessions. "For the full-day workshop, I spend the first one-and-a-half hours talking about applying reference techniques to your search strategies,"[24] he says.

> "It takes only one or two pages of Google hits to overwhelm the average reader. Does it really matter whether there are hundreds of thousands more pages after those?"[18]
>
> — Harvard University history professor Ann Blair.

Just two decades ago the Internet included a few dozen nontechnical websites. As the potential of the web started to materialize, a handful of visionaries saw that the key to using the Internet could be found in organizing the vast amounts of information that would soon become available online. Search engines such as Google or those available on specific sites, such as Amazon.com, have made it possible for people with very little knowledge about how the Internet works to find what they need—or at least come close to finding what they need. Clearly, though, as the amount and nature of information available on the Internet changes, Internet searchers will be faced with new challenges when it comes to sifting through a trove of websites that now numbers nearly 130 million.

Chapter Two

How Reliable Is Information Found Online?

During the 1960s John Seigenthaler Sr. worked as an aide to US attorney general Robert F. Kennedy, brother of President John F. Kennedy. President Kennedy was assassinated in 1963; five years later, while campaigning for the presidency, Robert Kennedy was also assassinated.

Four decades after the Kennedy assassinations, Seigenthaler was shocked to learn that for a time he was considered a suspect in the murders. He learned of his alleged involvement in the crimes by reading his biography on Wikipedia, the online encyclopedia, which said, "John Seigenthaler Sr. was the assistant to Attorney General Robert Kennedy in the early 1960s. For a brief time, he was thought to have been directly involved in the Kennedy assassinations of both John, and his brother, Bobby. Nothing was ever proven."[25]

In addition to suggesting that he played a role in two horrific crimes, the Wikipedia page also reported that following the murders, Seigenthaler hid for more than a decade in the former Soviet Union, evidently to remain out of reach of American law enforcement. "I have no idea whose sick mind conceived the false, malicious 'biography' that appeared under my name for 132 days on Wikipedia, the popular, online, free encyclopedia whose authors are unknown and virtually untraceable," says Seigenthaler. "At age 78, I thought I was beyond surprise or hurt at anything negative said about me. I was wrong. One sentence in the biography was true. I was Robert Kennedy's administrative assistant in the early 1960s. I also was his pallbearer."[26]

Online Activities by Age

Ages 18–33	Ages 34–45	Ages 46–55	Ages 56–64	Ages 65–73	Ages 74+
E-mail	E-mail	E-mail	E-mail	E-mail	E-mail
Search	Search	Search	Search	Search	Search
Health info	Health info	Health info	Health info	Health info	Health info
Social network sites	Get news	Get news	Get news	Get news	Buy a product
Watch video	Gov't website	Gov't website	Gov't website	Travel reservations	Get news
Get news	Travel reservations	Travel reservations	Buy a product	Buy a product	Travel reservations
Buy a product	Watch video	Buy a product	Travel reservations	Gov't website	Gov't website
IM	Buy a product	Watch video	Bank online	Watch video	Bank online
Listen to music	Social network sites	Bank online	Watch video	Financial info	Financial info
Travel reservations	Bank online	Social network sites	Social network sites	Bank online	Religious info
Online classifieds	Online classifieds	Online classifieds	Online classifieds	Rate things	Watch video
Bank online	Listen to music	Listen to music	Financial info	Social network sites	Play games
Gov't website	IM	Financial info	Rate things	Online classifieds	Online classifieds
Play games	Play games	IM	Listen to music	IM	Social network sites
Read blogs	Financial info	Religious info	Religious info	Religious info	Rate things
Financial info	Religious info	Rate things	IM	Play games	Read blogs
Rate things	Read blogs	Read blogs	Play games	Ilsten to music	Donate to charity
Religious info	Rate things	Play games	Read blogs	Read blogs	Listen to music
Online auction	Online auction	Online auction	Online auction	Donate to charity	Podcasts
Podcasts	Donate to charity	Donate to charity	Donate to charity	Online auction	Online auction
Donate to charity	Podcasts	Podcasts	Podcasts	Podcasts	Blog
Blog	Blog	Blog	Blog	Blog	IM
Virtual worlds	Virtual worlds	Virtual worlds	Virtual worlds	Virtual worlds	Virtual worlds

Source: Pew Internet & American Life Project, "Generations 2010: What Different Generations Do Online," December 16, 2010. www.pewinternet.org.

From Very Good to Very Bad

The Seigenthaler case illustrates the hazards of relying on sources like Wikipedia for serious scholarly research. Had a student assigned to write a paper on the Kennedy assassinations used Wikipedia as a source, that student would most certainly have received a failing grade.

The Internet may have made vast sources of information available to people, but the truth is that such information is subject to few controls. Indeed, for the most part the only people who are responsible for ensuring that the information posted on the Internet is accurate and objective are the people who post information on the Internet.

Says Robert Harris, a former college English professor and author who has written guidebooks for students on how to use the Internet,

> Information is everywhere on the Internet, existing in large quantities and continuously being created and revised. This information exists in a large variety of kinds (facts, opinions, stories, interpretations, statistics) and is created for many purposes (to inform, to persuade, to sell, to present a viewpoint, and to create or change an attitude or belief). For each of these various kinds and purposes, information exists on many levels of quality and reliability. It ranges from very good to very bad and includes every shade in between.[27]

Tests of Credibility

The challenge for students, researchers, and others seeking information on the Internet is to determine what constitutes good information and what does not. In reality, the chore of determining the accuracy and legitimacy of information is not much different than it was before the arrival of the Internet—whether it was found in books, periodicals, or other printed matter. If the author has the credentials to serve as an authority on the topic, and if the author's work has been vetted for accuracy by editors or other independent experts, readers can generally take comfort in knowing the information is legitimate. "Where did this information come from?" asks Harris. "What sources did the information creator use? Are the sources listed? Is there a bibliography or other documentation?"[28]

Those standards apply to Internet sites. Experts counsel Internet searchers to always consider the source of the information: Is the author of the content identified, along with his or her credentials to speak authoritatively on the issue? Is the content footnoted, giving readers an opportunity to assess the credibility of the information on their own? Does the sponsor of the website have an ulterior motive for presenting the information? Says author and Internet search consultant Wendy Boswell,

> Judging the truthfulness of information that you find online can be difficult at times. Fiction and reality are not the same thing, but on the Web it's sometimes hard to tell the difference: for example, there are many sites that claim to have rock-solid evidence that the Holocaust in World War II did not actually happen. If you didn't know any better, you might come across one of these very well-done, scholarly-appearing Web sites and think that they were speaking the truth.[29]

Altered by Outsiders

Clearly, in the Wikipedia biography of Seigenthaler, elements of credibility were largely missing. Wikipedia articles are written by anonymous authors whose work is generally not edited, fact-checked, or otherwise reviewed by independent experts. Such loose controls on the content meant that a prankster—perhaps somebody bearing a personal grudge against Seigenthaler—could gain access to the Wikipedia page and do mischief.

Originally, "wiki" was the name of a software tool that enables anyone to add or change content on a website. The term has since taken on a wider meaning, essentially referring to any website that can be altered by outsiders. On wiki sites the content is user-generated.

In 2000 Jimmy Wales, a former financial analyst from San Diego, California, attempted to establish an online encyclopedia that would include articles written by scholars and be vetted for accuracy by other scholars—essentially as any published encyclopedia is produced. The

How Accurate Is Wikipedia?

After hearing many complaints about the inaccuracies of the general information website Wikipedia, *Nature* magazine decided to examine the site's accuracy in contrast to the venerable *Encyclopaedia Britannica*. In 2005 *Nature* selected 42 articles on scientific topics that could be found on Wikipedia and compared them to the information found on the same topics in the *Encyclopaedia Britannica*. After reviewing the two sources, the authors of the *Nature* article concluded that Wikipedia made four errors for every three errors committed by the encyclopedia.

Officials at Wikipedia welcomed the comparison and suggested the survey illustrated the legitimacy of information found on the online encyclopedia. The publisher of the *Encyclopaedia Britannica* greeted the *Nature* survey with far less enthusiasm. "*Britannica* has never claimed to be error free," the encyclopedia's publisher said in a statement. "We have a reputation not for unattainable perfection but for strong scholarship, sound judgment, and disciplined editorial review." None of those factors, the *Britannica* publisher stated, are applied in the drafting of Wikipedia articles.

Quoted in Stacy Schiff, "Know It All," *New Yorker*, July 31, 2006, p. 36.

name of that project was Nupedia. After a year of attracting little interest among scholars in the online encyclopedia, Wales learned about the wiki software tool and decided to adopt it for his project. Within a year 20,000 articles had been posted on the website, which Wales named Wikipedia.

Concern to Educators

The growth of Wikipedia has been stunning. By 2011 anonymous volunteer contributors had posted more than 3.5 million articles on Wikipedia. Some of the entries are written by legitimate historians and other experts, but many are written by amateurs. Wikipedia, which is a project administered by a nonprofit organization known as Wikimedia, survives on grants and donations. It employs just a handful of paid staff members. Virtually all the workers are hired for their expertise in technology. None are responsible for fact-checking or otherwise confirming the information on the pages.

In contrast, the *Encyclopaedia Britannica*—long regarded as the gold standard in reference book publishing—included just some 120,000 entries in its latest printed edition, which was released in 2009. Moreover, the encyclopedia's publishers employ a staff of about 100 professionals to write and edit the entries, and most hold scholarly degrees and other credentials.

> "Judging the truthfulness of information that you find online can be difficult at times. Fiction and reality are not the same thing, but on the Web it's sometimes hard to tell the difference."[29]
>
> — Author and Internet search consultant Wendy Boswell.

Despite the lack of authenticity found on Wikipedia, the online encyclopedia still receives nearly 28 million visits a day from Internet users—a fact that is of considerable concern to educators. Indeed, many schools and colleges have banned Wikipedia use by students. Says Michael Gorman, former president of the American Library Association, "The problem with an online encyclopedia created by anybody is that you have no idea whether you are reading an established person in the field or someone with an ax to grind."[30]

In recent years Wikipedia has taken steps to establish vetting procedures. Volunteers serve on committees that regularly police the site for blatant falsehoods, obscenities, gags, and other abuses. Wikipedia also employs software that scans the pages for vandalism, such as mass deletions. "To me, the key thing is getting it right," says Wales. "I don't care if [contributors] are a high school kid or a Harvard professor."[31]

Dedication to Accuracy and Objectivity

Unlike Wikipedia, the information posted on the websites maintained by the mainstream media is subject to extensive editing and fact-checking. In fact, most newspaper websites are largely just online versions of the print editions of the papers delivered to doorsteps in the towns and cities where they circulate. Many of the sites do have some added components, such as links to videos of news events or interactive features that permit readers to add their comments to the ends of the stories, but the main features of most newspaper websites—the stories they publish—are the same stories that appear in print.

Even at small-circulation newspapers, stories written by journalists typically go through several hands before they are published in print or posted online. In addition to reviewing the stories for proper grammar, punctuation, and spelling, editors read the stories with an eye toward weeding out inaccuracies and bias. It is not unusual for some stories to be submitted to an attorney who determines whether the articles are libelous, meaning the stories exhibit a reckless disregard for the truth. Only after the stories pass muster through the newspaper's internal editing procedures are they cleared to be published in print or online. Articles posted online by local and national TV and radio news staffs are similarly vetted for accuracy and fairness.

Although newspapers and other traditional news outlets do make mistakes, their stories undergo several stages of editing (as shown here) and sometimes are even sent for legal review to avoid inaccuracies and bias. News blog content generally does not go through this process.

Clearly, readers appreciate this degree of dedication to accuracy and objectivity. In 2010 the Newspaper Association of America (NAA)—a trade group representing American newspaper publishers—surveyed 3,000 Internet users to find out where they find their news online. The NAA also wanted to know the degree of trust those readers place on the news they read. The study showed that a majority of the respondents—57 percent—head first to the websites maintain by newspapers and, moreover, many of the respondents find the news they read on those sites to be accurate and unbiased. "This survey reinforces the notion that consumers value and trust the premium quality content found at newspaper websites,"[32] says Randy Bennett, senior vice president of the NAA.

Bloggers: Citizen Journalists

But not all news found online is posted there by professional journalists or news staffs. In addition to these mainstream media outlets, the Internet serves as home to tens of thousands of blogs. (The term *blog* was originally an abbreviation for "web log" but is now so common that it generally stands by itself.)

While many blogs are written by mainstream journalists—usually as features that appear on their newspapers' websites—many bloggers regard themselves as "citizen journalists." They may have no training in journalism, but they do have something to say. And since they also have the wherewithal to maintain websites, bloggers are able to find outlets for their opinions. In many cases, bloggers intentionally blur the lines between fact and opinion, meaning that an unsuspecting reader who finds his or her way to a blogger's website may not realize that the news posted on the site is fraught with inaccuracies and biases.

"The problem with an online encyclopedia created by anybody is that you have no idea whether you are reading an established person in the field or someone with an ax to grind."[30]

— Michael Gorman, former president of the American Library Association.

Moreover, the information found on blogs is often picked up, along with the sites maintained by the mainstream media, in searches performed through Google and other search engines. Google features a news filter, meaning Internet users can narrow their searches to news stories only. It means that bloggers can see their commentaries listed on the Google organic lists alongside stories published by the *New York Times*, *Washington Post*, and other mainstream news organizations.

Birth of the Blogs

As with most content found on the Internet, blogs originally covered technical matters. The first blogs were posted in the early 1990s, written by computer engineers as a mode of sharing technical information with other engineers. The spark that truly ignited the blogosphere was the adoption by Congress in 1996 of the US Communications Decency Act. It was an attempt by Congress to regulate the content of information posted online. The main intent of the legislation was to bar access to Internet pornography by children and teenagers, but free speech advocates worried that the law could be applied to virtually any form of expression. Opponents of the act believed the measure violated the First Amendment right to free speech. As the measure was debated in Washington, software designer Dave Winer established *24 Hours of Democracy*, the first blog devoted to a political issue, specifically opposition to the Communications Decency Act.

> "To me, the key thing is getting it right. I don't care if [contributors] are a high school kid or a Harvard professor."[31]
>
> — Wikipedia founder Jimmy Wales.

Winer used the blog to keep his readers updated on developments in Congress but also invited others to contribute to the blog, prompting responses by dozens of readers. Among the contributors to Winer's blog was Bill Gates, the founder of Microsoft, who contributed an essay calling for free speech on the Internet. "If [the act] is allowed to stand, it will undermine our nation's Bill of Rights—and there is no question that it will interfere with the ability of the Internet to flourish. It is so restrictive that it will scare people who fear they might commit a felony, by simply discussing a controversial topic,"[33] wrote Gates.

The act was tossed out in 1997 by the US Supreme Court, which agreed with the bloggers—that the act violated the First Amendment. And although the bloggers really had no impact on the actual challenge to the law—the case against the measure was argued in court by the American Civil Liberties Union—Winer showed how a blog could be used to sway public opinion.

Is the Information Authoritative?

It did not take long for all manner of blogs to emerge on the web. In the years since *24 Hours of Democracy* made its debut, tens of thousands of other bloggers have established Internet pages where they discuss cooking, travel, auto repair, medical issues, pet care, music, celebrities, professional athletes, and hundreds of other topics. Many are interactive, giving readers opportunities to post comments as well. "I have a personal blog in which I write about my daily life with my family, my cats, and life in general," says Boswell. "Sure, it's probably not interesting to anyone but me, but it's got that all important element of 'people' in it."[34]

Some blogs provide authoritative information. Martha Stewart has been guiding homeowners with tips on house decor, gardening, cooking, and style for decades—mostly in her books, magazine, and on her TV show. She also makes use of the Internet to connect to her fans, writing a blog providing helpful tips. Professional football quarterback Donovan McNabb keeps his fans informed on his career and activities through his personal blog, which he has titled Yardbarker. Fans of pop star Miley Cyrus can read blog entries from the singer on her official website. Certainly, considering the sources, the information provided by Boswell as well as Stewart, McNabb, and Cyrus is bona fide and available for reading by anybody with Internet access.

However, other blogs do not provide information that can be regarded in any description as authoritative. Since most blogs operate under the same rules that guide much of the content on the web—they are not edited or vetted for accuracy and objectivity by independent experts—critics caution people to be wary of the content found in the blogosphere. "Blogs are personal," says Dave Warlick, a school technology consultant. "They are one way for an individual to express personal beliefs with a certain amount of personality. So there are probably as many ways that a blog can look and read as there are blogs."[35]

Coloring the News

When it comes to blogs that specialize in reporting the news or commenting on the news, many zealous bloggers will allow their personal beliefs to color the news that appears on their websites. Markos Moulitas is a well-known blogger whose commentaries on his DailyKos.com blog

Online Hysteria and the
Deepwater Horizon

Newspapers may receive high marks for the accuracy of the information they post online, but many newspapers also give space on their websites to bloggers. In some cases, newspaper bloggers have been responsible for spreading hysteria and false information.

Shortly after the *Deepwater Horizon* oil rig exploded in the Gulf of Mexico in 2010, spilling millions of gallons of oil into the environment, federal authorities elected to disperse the oil by using a chemical known as Corexit 9500. Their hope was that the dispersant would break up the oil slick into tiny droplets, making it easier for the environment to absorb the oil. Critics of the plan contended that Corexit 9500 contained hazardous ingredients and could do more harm than good.

As the Corexit 9500 was sprayed onto the slick, a blogger posted this entry on the website of the *San Francisco Chronicle*: "I was disturbed to get another anonymous tip that Corexit 9500 also has dihydrogen monoxide." The blogger added that dihydrogen monoxide is "really bad and nasty stuff."

Dihydrogen monoxide is, in actuality, pretty tame stuff. It is recognized mostly by its chemical symbol, H_2O, and is otherwise known by its more common name: water.

Quoted in Raffi Khatchadourian, "The Gulf War," *New Yorker*, March 14, 2011, p. 53.

attract some 600,000 visitors a day. Moulitas makes no secret of his liberal bias and often uses his blog to attack Republican politicians and other conservatives. On the other side of the political spectrum, conservatives can get their fill of liberal-bashing on the blogs authored by Michelle Malkin, whose MichelleMalkin.com and HotAir.com sites attract more than 200,000 visitors a day.

Members of the mainstream media acknowledge that conservatives and liberals may be able to find very readable commentaries about politics on such sites, but what readers do not find on those sites is objective news reporting. They insist that reports written by bloggers are usually biased and do not present a fair and balanced view of the news. Former CBS news correspondent Eric Engberg compares the content found on blogs to the mind-numbing chatter heard over the airwaves during the 1970s when Citizen Band radios were all the rage. "The public is now assaulted by news and pretend-news from many directions, thanks to the now infamous 'information superhighway.' But the ability to transmit words, we learned during the Citizens Band radio fad of the 70s, does not mean that any knowledge is being passed along," he says. "The chances of the bloggers replacing mainstream journalism are about as good as the parasite replacing the dog it fastens on."[36]

> "The public is now assaulted by news and pretend-news from many directions, thanks to the now infamous 'information superhighway.'"[36]
>
> — Former CBS news correspondent Eric Engberg.

And MSNBC producer Joan Connell points out that blogs often suffer from the same credibility gap that Wikipedia faces—no independent critical eye reads the content of the blog before it is posted on the Internet, where it has the potential to reach tens of millions of readers. "I would submit that the editing function really is the factor that makes it journalism," says Connell. "Are you making a mistake here? Do you really want to say that? Do you really want to use that word? Is that libelous?"[37]

Many bloggers argue that blogs were never intended as outlets for fair and unbiased reporting. They see themselves as providing an important public service—presenting news and opinion as only the Internet can: in a version that is unedited and uncensored. Says Scott Knowles, who maintains a blog that focuses on online access issues, "It's really what the web is all about . . . each person having their own voice, and really kind of a democratization of media."[38]

Rating Trustworthy Websites

Internet users who want to assess the legitimacy of blogs and other websites do have places to turn. A number of organizations post lists of the Internet's most accurate and trusted websites. Among the organizations that rate the trustworthiness of websites are the nonprofit groups 100bestwebsites.org and SearchEngineWatch.com. Also, *Forbes* magazine posts lists of websites that it has found to contain the most accurate and objective information. Typically, these sites list categories—such as business, the arts, medical issues, and news—giving a critique of the sites within those categories.

For example, 100bestwebsites.org listed two medical-related sites—NIH.gov and MayoClinic.com—among its top 25 sites on the Internet. NIH.gov is maintained by the National Institutes of Health, a federal agency, while MayoClinic.com is maintained by the Mayo Clinic of Rochester, Minnesota, which is considered one of the country's foremost hospitals. "Simply put, the Mayo Clinic is one of the greatest hospitals and medical research centers on planet earth," says 100bestwebsites.org. "In that tradition, the Mayo Clinic provides this excellent website devoted to promotion of human health."[39]

> "[Blogs are] really what the web is all about . . . each person having their own voice, and really kind of a democratization of media."[38]
>
> — Blogger Scott Knowles.

Another group that rates the quality of websites is the International Academy of Digital Arts and Sciences which, like its counterparts in the film, TV, and music industries, confers awards on the top achievers in digital arts. These prizes are known as the Webby Awards.

The academy makes awards in dozens of categories. Many honor art design and technical achievements, but some awards are devoted to the presentation of accurate and trusted information. For example, the 2010 Webby Award winner for education was wechoosethemoon.org, which chronicled the 1969 flight of *Apollo 11*, the first manned spacecraft to land on the moon.

Assessing the Value of Online Information

Organizations such as 100bestwebsites.org, SearchEngineWatch.com, and the International Academy of Digital Arts and Sciences serve an important role in steering people toward websites they can trust because the government has little role in judging the accuracy of what is found on the web. Indeed, other than establishing laws guarding against libel and the distribution of child pornography, the government generally stays

The International Academy of Digital Arts and Sciences recognizes websites that provide high-quality, accurate information. The group's 2010 Webby Award went to a site that chronicled the 1969 Apollo 11 *moon mission. Pictured is astronaut Edwin "Buzz" Aldrin deploying scientific equipment on the moon during that mission.*

out of the debate over what defines trustworthy web content. Congress learned its lesson following the Supreme Court decision that tossed out the Communications Decency Act. In the years following the Supreme Court decision, legislators have made no other attempts to draft laws regulating Internet content.

That means the only people who decide whether the information found on the Internet is reliable, accurate, and objective are the people who put it there. Members of the mainstream media edit articles, vet them for accuracy, and sometimes even obtain clearance from lawyers if they harbor doubts about the legality of the information they intend to publish, broadcast, or post online. On the other hand, many bloggers, Wikipedia authors, and others have their own ideas about how to present information on the Internet. In the final analysis, the burden seems to fall mostly on the readers of Internet content to assess the value of the information they find online.

Chapter Three

The Business of Search and Information

Derek Jeter is one of baseball's most recognizable and popular stars. He has played shortstop for the New York Yankees since 1995 and, since then, has been a perennial all-star. In the world of online searching, though, Jeter means much more. To Gatorade, the makers of the sports energy drink G2, the Yankees shortstop represented a golden marketing opportunity.

In 2008, as Gatorade prepared to introduce G2 to the marketplace, the company paid Google for the rights to the keywords "Derek Jeter." For several months, whenever a baseball fan entered the words "Derek Jeter" into the Google search engine, a small advertisement promoting G2 would pop up on the screen alongside the organic results. Why would the makers of G2 desire their product to be promoted alongside Internet search inquiries into the life and career of Derek Jeter? "Gatorade wanted to align itself with successful athletes—the types of people its audiences look up to and aspire to be,"[40] says Internet marketing expert Aaron Goldman.

In other words, Gatorade knew that the type of people who would ordinarily seek information on Jeter are the same type of people who might play baseball themselves or otherwise pursue active lifestyles. To help market its new sports drink, Gatorade wanted to introduce the brand during a period when people are highly susceptible to new ideas—a time when they are actually looking for information by searching the Internet. Says Goldman, "When people are searching, they have their antennae up and

Online information has become big business. Gatorade paid Google for the rights to the keywords "Derek Jeter" so that when someone did a search on the New York Yankees shortstop (pictured), an advertisement promoting G2 would pop up on the screen beside the search results.

are open to outside offers from third parties. Someone searching for Jeter may just be looking for baseball scores, but, because they're in between Web sites, they're more open to being steered in a new direction."[41]

Screen Presence

The promotion of G2 illustrates how companies have learned to tie their fortunes to the search for information on the Internet. Gatorade tied its marketing directly to Google searching, but other companies have devised other strategies. Many companies craft the text on their websites specifically to attract consumers making web searches. Others go so far as to make decisions on what type of inventory to stock based on the popularity of keywords employed in Internet searches.

Search engines like Google may provide millions of users a day with the information they are seeking about Jeter or how and why George Washington crossed the Delaware River or a multitude of other topics, but in reality these companies earn their profits by selling advertising. The fact that Google can charge advertisers to link their promotions to keywords illustrates the monetary value of information on the Internet. Companies like Gatorade are willing to pay in order to have a presence on computer screens at a time when the owners of those screens—consumers—are

seeking that information. Indeed, in 2010 Google earned $20 billion through the sales of advertisements.

Most of the ads that appear on Google are the so-called "AdSense" ads, like those that Gatorade ran to promote G2. These ads are limited to 95 characters, but they magically pop up along the right side of the screen whenever a user punches in the keywords bought by the company.

> **"When people are searching, they have their antennae up and are open to outside offers from third parties."[41]**
>
> — Internet marketing expert Aaron Goldman.

For example, a homeowner who enters the keywords "clothes dryer" into the Google search bar will see a list of organic sites explaining the functions and maintenance of clothes dryers, but the consumer will also see AdSense promotions for clothes dryers sold by Sears or the Home Depot. Likewise, people searching for information on car insurance may see AdSense advertisements placed by the car insurance companies GEICO or State Farm. Says Goldman, "Google ads perform well because they reach people in a commercial mindset."[42]

Search Engine Optimization

Despite the large numbers, advertising represents only a small share of the e-commerce conducted over the Internet. In 2011 Forrester Research, a Cambridge, Massachusetts–based market research firm, reported that the amount of goods and services sold over the Internet to

American consumers totaled nearly $200 billion. By 2015, the firm suggests, online retail commerce in America could reach nearly $280 billion. Meanwhile, in Europe, Forrester reported online sales of $125 billion in 2011 and projects as much as $183 billion by 2015. Online commerce in Asian countries, particularly China, is also robust. In 2011 the Shanghai, China–based market research company DDMA reported that the Chinese spend $82 billion a year in online commerce.

Much of that money changes hands when consumers buy goods or services online from vendors such as Amazon or shoes and apparel retailer Zappos or computer maker Dell. These companies and many others have invested millions of dollars into crafting their websites so that they will attract users who are led to their sites through Internet searches. This practice is known as search engine optimization, or SEO. It is also known as "keyword stuffing."

> "You can confidently presume that we are leading the way in finding an [economic] model that maximizes returns. . . . The current days of the Internet will soon be over." [48]
>
> — Rupert Murdoch, head of the media conglomerate that publishes the *Wall Street Journal* and *New York Post*.

Indeed, many companies have identified words that they know are among the most popular search terms used on the various search engines. Apparel companies, in particular, know the words that work best. According to WordStream, a Boston, Massachusetts, marketing company, the five most common keywords employed by Internet users in searches for apparel are "fashion," "women fashion," "vintage fashion," "retro fashion" and "shoes fashion."

The challenge for Internet marketing professionals is to work those keywords into the texts of their web pages so that when a consumer performs a search using those keywords, their clients' sites will surface at or near the top of the organic results. Says Simon Hollingsworth, lead researcher for Greenlight, a British marketing agency, "In terms of keywords, it is all well and good having a great website but unless you are optimizing the right words then you are missing out on opportunities." [43]

Keywords Mean Business

SEO is an ongoing process. Many companies study search and sales trends and have determined the best times of the week—or even the best times

Google's Sponsored Links

People who use Google cannot help but notice the small 95-character ads that appear on the right side of the pages that display the search results. Other ads appear on the page as well. These ads are known as Sponsored Links. They appear above the lists of organic search results.

At first glance, Sponsored Links seem to be ordinary search results. Other than appearing in a colored background (usually pink), the ads invite Internet users to click on their links for more information. Nevertheless, Sponsored Links are paid ads, and Google has intentionally made them to resemble noncommercial organic results.

Studies have shown that many people cannot tell the difference between paid ads on Google and noncommercial search results. A study by the Pew Internet & American Life Project found that 60 percent of Google searchers cannot tell the difference between paid ads and nonpaid organic listings. Says author Alejandro M. Diaz, an expert on online marketing, "Even though these are also labeled as 'sponsored,' selected by relevance, not price, and appear over a colored background, the fact remains: a considerable portion of Google's revenue comes from moving ads to the most prominent positions above the 'first hit.' It is unclear whether, in practice, users perceive these as ads."

Alejandro M. Diaz, "Through the Google Goggles: Sociopolitical Bias in Search Engine Design," in Amanda Spink and Michael T. Zimmer, eds., *Web Search: Multidisciplinary Perspectives*. Berlin, Germany: Springer, 2008, p. 22.

of day—to use certain keywords on their home pages. In Great Britain, for example, studies of Internet use have determined that most women trawl the Internet for apparel sales on Sundays and weekday evenings. To take advantage of the traffic, they change their keywords during the times when they know most customers will be looking for deals on clothes. "A lot of companies are still unaware of the opportunities available," says Hollingsworth. "Keyword targeting is important for [search]. To create the right campaigns it is important to understand how your consumers search through the buying cycle."[44]

Some businesses invest in new products after they discover a desire for those products through research on keyword use. Goldman points to the example of Diamond Tour Golf, a DeKalb, Illinois, company that sells golfing equipment. The company discovered that among the most frequent keywords used on Google by golfers were "left-handed" and "junior." Diamond Tour Golf did not offer products for left-handed or young players, so the company quickly added that equipment to its inventory. "Sure enough," says Goldman, "the company began to carry these type of clubs, and they quickly became top sellers."[45]

A More Subtle Approach

When companies stuff their websites with carefully chosen keywords, they do so with the intention of pitching products to potential buyers. Their whole websites are essentially interactive advertisements offering graphics, text, and video that help explain the products for sale.

Other companies try a much more subtle approach. They lure Internet users to their websites with the promise of providing information, but also find ways to market their products while they have the attention of the users. An example of this approach is the website Beinggirl.com, which is sponsored by the huge consumer products company Proctor & Gamble (P&G).

The company set up the website as a resource for teenage girls, supplying them with information on issues that might interest teenage girls such as how to deal with stress, what to do about cyberbullies, and how to guard against identity theft. Articles are also posted about health issues, such as menstruation—as well as advertisements for the company's feminine hygiene products. "P&G is behind a large online community of teenage girls called Beinggirl.com where the consumer giant's products are effectively highlighted,"[46] says Internet marketing expert Robert L. Dilenschneider.

P&G is using a soft-sell approach. The website does not feature a hard sell in which the viewer is told he or she *absolutely* needs the product. Instead, when employing the Internet as a marketing tool, companies often present the visitor with the information he or she desires. Then, through a very subtle process visitors are reminded that the company has related products available on its website. Adds Dilenschneider, "A website is not only about transmitting information, advocating a cause, or selling a product or service. It's about communicating a presence or the compelling message about what the organization represents."[47]

The Cost of Information

Whether they use a hard sell or soft sell, these companies exploit consumers' desire for information to lure shoppers to their websites so that they may, ultimately, sell them products. In recent years, though, a new form of e-commerce has surfaced: Many companies are now charging for the information that consumers desire.

Charging for online information is certainly not new. Many scholarly journals publish online versions and assess fees on Internet users for access to their articles. Dating services require subscriptions—members have to pay for access to the databases of potential dates. And in recent years, some newspapers have decided to start charging readers who desire to view their content online.

In the 1990s, when most newspapers established their websites, they elected to post their news for free—and to support the cost of providing the news by selling web-based advertisements. That economic model has rarely proven to be profitable. Now, many newspaper publishers have concluded that the news they publish is their most precious commodity and are no longer willing to give it away for free.

> "Imagine a world where some students have more resources [than] others, and students in college can't access what they need to for research projects, where some schools can't have [the] Internet because the package they need is too expensive."[51]
>
> — Keith Whistler, a student from Elmhurst, Illinois.

The news stories are still available online; now, though, the Internet users are sometimes charged a fee—usually about $2—to gain access to a single story. Internet users also have the option of paying weekly or monthly fees that give them unlimited access to the newspaper's website. In most cases, subscribers to the print editions are given free access to online content. Says Rupert Murdoch, head of the media conglomerate that publishes the *Wall Street Journal* and *New York Post*, "You can confidently presume that we are leading the way in finding an [economic] model that maximizes returns. . . . The current days of the Internet will soon be over."[48]

Blame the Internet

Many newspaper publishers insist that they have no alternative but to charge for online news. During the past decade, according to the NAA, nearly 100 daily newspapers have gone out of business, while those that remain have seen significant drops in their paid circulations. The NAA reports that between 2000 and 2009, paid circulation at all American daily newspapers dropped by more than 10 million readers.

Most publishers blame the Internet, believing that access to free news has hurt their paid circulations. Says Joshua Benton, director of the Nieman Journalism Lab at Harvard University in Massachusetts, "News executives are starting to recognize that online advertising revenues are not enough on their own."[49]

While some newspaper executives believe they can earn healthy profits by selling the news to customers on the web, others believe the interest among Internet users in buying the news is minimal. Benton estimates that just 3 percent of people who have been visiting newspaper websites will be interested in paying for the news they have previously been getting for free.

Instead, many publishers predict their paid circulations will start rising once people learn they have to pay for web access. Says Tyler Patton, publisher of the *Valley Morning Star* in Harlingen, Texas, "It will allow greater value to our many loyal print-edition subscribers by not giving away the news to nonsubscribers."[50]

Net Neutrality

As newspaper publishers and other businesspeople mull over ways to turn information into profit, what is clear is that none of that information would be available to any user without the infrastructure to deliver the Internet to hundreds of millions of users. In recent years, the companies that maintain that infrastructure have concluded that they should no longer bear the cost of delivering the information.

The Challenges of Search Engine Optimization

Search engine optimization (SEO) is the use of keywords in the text of a website to help a site surface near the top of search engine results. A business that can place its site at the top of the results will have a better opportunity of attracting consumers than a site that places well down in the results.

SEO is hardly an exact science. Debenhams, a London-based apparel company, discovered that many women visit the company's website while they are working, often during their lunch hours. To lure those consumers to its site, Debenhams employs keywords such as "Jasper Conran" and "Red Herring"—the names of popular British apparel makers. Typically, Debenhams changes the text of its site so those keywords appear during noon hour.

However, Debenhams has also learned that many of those customers do not buy clothes during their lunch breaks. Instead, they return later in the evening to make the purchases. It means that Debenhams cannot rely on those keywords during the noon-time shopping hours to help draw shoppers. Says Jo Stephenson, a senior marketing manager for Debenhams, "If someone was searching in the office for dresses at lunchtime, then they might go home and buy it online. But we'll never match the sale back to the keyword they first started searching for."

Quoted in Lucy Handley, "Maximize Your Search Appeal," *Marketing Week*, December 2, 2010, p. 23.

These companies are telecommunications corporations that provide phone lines and wireless networks capable of delivering huge amounts of information. The lines and networks must accommodate wide bandwidth, which is the ability to transmit data. In America, companies such as Verizon and AT&T own the networks and deliver information. In European nations as well as other countries, government-owned companies typically provide the service.

To help finance the cost of maintaining modern phone lines and networks, the telecommunications companies have proposed that the information providers—such as Google and Bing—share in the cost. At issue is so-called net neutrality—whether all content should be made available to every Internet user on a fair, equal, and neutral basis.

The implication of the demands by the telecommunications companies is significant. If they charge for the right to ship content over their telephone lines and wireless networks, the search engines could simply decide it is not worth the cost. They could elect not to provide content that would demand a high bandwidth. They may even elect to stop providing service over networks that demand high fees.

Other content providers—generally anyone who offers users access to games, MP3 files, videos, and other data that require a lot of bandwidth—would be similarly charged for their content. Such charges could have

The Denver Post *documents the demise of the* Rocky Mountain News— *one of many newspapers that have folded in recent years. Panicked by such failures and the popularity of online news, many newspapers made their content available for free online. Some are beginning to rethink that decision.*

wide-ranging implications for Internet users because the fees would almost
certainly be passed on to consumers: If students researching term papers
find they have to pay fees for information, would they opt for cheaper—
and perhaps less accurate—sources of data?
Would budget-conscious schools and colleges seek the cheapest, but not necessarily
the most complete, providers of Internet
content? Says Keith Whistler, a student
from Elmhurst, Illinois, "Imagine a world
where some students have more resources
[than] others, and students in college can't
access what they need to for research projects, where some schools can't have [the] Internet because the package they need is too
expensive. Well, without net neutrality we are going to hinder our youths'
future, and make their education harder, and definitely more expensive."[51]

> "I believe we are
> facing and will
> continue to face a
> growing threat of
> corporate control
> on the flow of
> information in our
> country."[52]
>
> — US senator Al Franken of Min-
> nesota.

Removing US Government Control

Supporters of net neutrality also argue that if Verizon, AT&T, and others
can assess fees, they will add charges and roadblocks that have nothing to
do with enlarging bandwidth. They argue that the telecommunications
companies could possibly stop or slow down content in order to gain an
advantage over competitors. For example, critics point out that the cable
TV giant Comcast, which provides Internet content over its cable lines,
purchased the NBC television network in 2011. Would Comcast find ways
to block Internet sites by NBC's competitors? Said US senator Al Franken
of Minnesota, "I believe we are facing and will continue to face a growing
threat of corporate control on the flow of information in our country."[52]

In America AT&T, Verizon, and other telecommunications companies have spent years lobbying the Federal Communications Commission (FCC) to permit them to start charging fees, but in late 2010 the
FCC voted to maintain net neutrality. The issue is not likely to go away.
In Washington some congressional leaders oppose government control
over any facet of private commerce, including e-commerce. They aim to
revisit the issue with the goal of removing all government control over
fees that telecommunications companies are permitted to charge. "The

Internet has grown and flourished without burdensome federal regulations, becoming an integral part of American society," says Senator Kay Bailey Hutchinson of Texas. "Internet-related innovation, strengthened by the free market, has spurred the development of new businesses, fueled job creation and has become a major part of America's day-to-day lives. . . . We must preserve the openness of the Internet without unnecessary government intervention."[53]

Fees Banned in Europe

Meanwhile, in Europe the government-run telecommunications companies also contend that information providers should be made to share in the cost of maintaining high bandwidth. "Internet search engines use our Net without paying anything at all, which is good for them and bad for us," complains César Alierta, the president of Telefónica, Spain's national telephone company. "It's obvious that this situation must change."[54]

> "The Internet has grown and flourished without burdensome federal regulations, becoming an integral part of American society. . . . We must preserve the openness of the Internet without unnecessary government intervention."[53]
>
> — Senator Kay Bailey Hutchinson of Texas.

The heads of several other European telecommunications companies joined Alierta in calling for fees on content providers. Said Stéphane Richard, chief executive of France Telecom, "There is something totally not normal and contrary to economic logic to let Google use our network without paying the price."[55]

As in the United States, the demands by the telecommunications executives were at least temporarily shelved when Neelie Kroes, the European Union commissioner for telecommunications, said she would ban fees on the search engines and other information providers. "Users should be able to access and distribute the content, services and applications they want,"[56] she said.

Primed for Growth

The debate over net neutrality is likely to surface again. As content providers find new ways to make information available to consumers, chances are the amount of bandwidth required to deliver that content will continue to rise. Upgrading phone lines and wireless networks to continue delivering that bandwidth is sure to be expensive, increasing the likelihood that the telecommunications companies will renew their calls for the content providers to share in the cost. How these new costs will affect consumers of information remains to be seen.

The cost of providing information is sure to rise in other ways. In 2011 the *New York Times* announced plans to charge for access to its website, NYTimes.com. At the time the venerable newspaper publisher established fees for online access, the website was the most popular news source on the Internet with some 17 million visitors a month. In the coming years, other newspaper publishers are expected to charge for Internet access as well. Eventually, the amount of free news available on the Internet could be dramatically reduced.

Meanwhile, advertisements will continue to pop up during Google searches, while shoppers find themselves drawn to certain websites as the science of keyword stuffing becomes more refined. The business of delivering information on the Internet seems to be primed for growth.

Chapter Four

How Is Online Information Changing the Classroom?

Founded in 1968, Central Florida University in Orlando is a relatively new college. Over the years, the university's student enrollment has continued to shoot skyward, leaving the school with a chronic shortage of classroom space. In recent years, though, Central Florida has found a way to provide courses to students without the need to erect expensive classroom buildings: The school has established an abundant number of online classes.

It means students can view lectures, access research materials, and even take tests from their desks in their dorm rooms. Moreover, they can "attend" class whenever their schedules allow—even late at night. A typical online student at Central Florida is Ariel Hatten, a junior nursing major, who earned credits studying medical terminology in an online class. Hatten preferred to take the class in a quiet study area of the student union center. Finding an empty desk, she set up her laptop and logged on to the class website where an assignment required her to match medical terms with body parts. Each time she dragged a term and placed it over the correct body part, the computer chimed. "It's wonderful."[57] she said.

A day later, Hatten attended a class in physiology where she sat through a lecture by a professor who droned on in a thick accent while showing slides to the class. Hatten admitted that sitting through the class can be a struggle. "She's really nice," the nursing student said of her professor, "but she doesn't teach very well."[58]

Staying Focused

Thanks to the Internet, students can obtain the same information in cyberspace that was previously available only in a classroom setting. More and more colleges, as well as high schools, have realized the advantages of what is known as "e-learning" or "distance learning" and are making online classes a part of their curricula.

In Missouri, for example, about 2,000 students have signed up for a pilot program that enables them to take all their classes online. One of the participants is Philip Marten, an eleventh-grade student from Shawnee, Missouri. The only time Marten steps foot in Shawnee Mission Northwest High School is to attend rehearsals of the school orchestra, where he plays violin. Otherwise, Marten takes all of his classes online.

A Virginia high school student works on an assignment from his online advanced placement calculus class. More and more high schools and colleges are offering e-learning classes.

Marten says online classes fit into his lifestyle. The student says that he has trouble staying focused late in the afternoon, so taking the classes when he feels at his sharpest has helped his academic performance. "I don't think I operate well in a public school situation,"[59] he says.

Another online student, Randall Haney, who attends Savannah College of Art and Design in Georgia, says he feels less pressure in online classes—he was able to complete his work at his own speed without having to worry about keeping up with others. "It's great to progress at my own pace,"[60] he says.

Many Distractions

While students like Marten and Haney can thrive in virtual classrooms, many experts believe online education has its pitfalls. For starters, school officials believe that some students would skip online assignments more often than they would skip assignments handed out in classrooms. "It's easy to get distracted while completing work online," says Katie Ruth Hinton, a 15-year-old student from Floydada, Texas, who has taken online computer technology courses. "You need . . . to keep yourself from playing games when you should be studying."[61]

Marten agrees that online students have to be highly motivated because no teachers are looking over their shoulders, ensuring that they complete their assignments. He says, "You don't always have the person there saying, 'Hey, this needs to be in now.'"[62]

Other students may find it easy to cheat. When administering tests in the classroom, most teachers do not permit students to open their notebooks or textbooks. But when taking a test at home or in a dorm room, who is to know? "No one enforces you to do the right thing," says Hatten. "It's at your discretion. I care about my grade so if I don't know the answer I'm not going to let myself fail when I have an opportunity to look in the book."[63]

Personal Interaction

What may be most lacking in online classes, though, is the personal interaction between teacher and student. Many teachers believe they have to see the students in their classrooms in order to engage them in the lessons—they need to look into the eyes of their students to ensure they are grasping the information. "Some kids really need to have a teacher in front of them,"[64] says Marla Walker, coordinator of online learning for the North Kansas City School District in Missouri.

Many students who take online courses insist, though, that teachers are available for one-on-one help when needed. Hillary Laaker, an eleventh-grade student from Linwood, Kansas, says that when she poses questions to teachers in e-mails, she finds their answers to be much more detailed and explanatory than the answers she would receive from teachers standing in the front of their classes. Teachers also respond to phone calls, she says. While working on an assignment over one weekend, Laaker says, she called a teacher and left a detailed message about a problem she encountered in the work. Laaker says she expected to receive an answer sometime on Monday, but instead the teacher called her back Sunday night. Laaker says the teacher was willing to stay on the phone for as long as Laaker needed help. "[My teachers] have such dedication to helping you do your best,"[65] she says.

> "The trend in online enrollments among US higher education institutions has been steadily upward: with growth rates for all years easily exceeding the growth in the overall higher education student body size."[68]
>
> — United States Distance Learning Association.

And Chelsea Lotman, a Florida student who took online courses as a high school sophomore, says her distance-learning class featured an Internet chat room where she could pose questions and receive feedback not only from the teacher but from other students. "I could speak with other students if we wanted to compare notes,"[66] she says.

Still, Walker also points out that even if online students do get a measure of personal attention from teachers, they risk missing out on all the other experiences that schools and colleges provide—the clubs and other extracurricular activities, the sports, and even the camaraderie of making friends and sharing good times with them.

An important part of going to school, Walker says, involves young people building relationships with others their own ages and learning how to act maturely in social situations. Students who spend all their time at home, staring at their laptop screens, lack those experiences, she says. "I really think it's good for [students] to have that social interaction with other students,"[67] says Walker.

Online learning has many benefits but some education experts say that students who take online courses risk missing out on relationship building and the other interpersonal experiences that come with participation in clubs, sports, and other on-campus activities.

Hybrid Courses

While students who take all their classes at home may be missing out on important school experiences, still more and more students are engaging in distance learning. According to the United States Distance Learning Association, online enrollment in American colleges grew from 1.6 million students in 2002 to more than 5.5 million in 2009. In addition, the association reports, the share of college students taking at least one course online grew from 10 percent in 2002 to nearly 30 percent in 2009. Says a report by the association, "The trend in online enrollments among US higher education institutions has been steadily upward: with growth rates for all years easily exceeding the growth in the overall higher education student body size. The evidence for past years has shown little, if any, indication that this growth is slowing."[68]

As more colleges and high schools offer online courses, students should not expect all of their classes to be conducted over the Internet. Most experts predict that schools will ultimately offer a combination of courses taught in traditional classroom settings as well as online classes and hybrids, in which some material will be offered online and some material presented in classroom lectures. Says Margie Martyn, coordinator of distance learning at Baldwin-Wallace College in Berea, Ohio, "The challenge is to find the optimal mix of online and face-to-face instruction that will leverage the major advantage of . . . learning (any time, any place), while still maintaining quality faculty-student interaction."[69]

Class Websites

Whether the material is taught online or in the classroom, many schools and school districts have established websites where students can find information such as homework assignments, due dates, grades, and contact information for their teachers. More sophisticated websites may include links to resources—such as study guides created by the teachers. Some websites may also provide links to outside sources that students can access to help them complete the assignments.

Some teachers post questions on their websites and require students to provide answers. Some websites include blogs where students can pose questions, giving other students the opportunities to help them find the answers. "These questions and answers can develop into deeper discussions than classroom time would allow," says Lemoyne S. Dunn, program coordinator for the Texas Center for Educational Technology. "They also sometimes reveal misconceptions [teachers] would not have otherwise discovered, making the class website a valuable formative assessment tool."[70]

> "I think it will help because you don't have to cut down as many trees. Think about that, how much paper is being used in those textbooks."[74]
>
> — Former California governor Arnold Schwarzenegger.

Parents can also find a class website helpful because the information found online can help them monitor their children's work. Some teachers have even established websites specifically for parents who want to monitor homework or test results or simply want a place where they can establish a dialogue with the teacher. "I have a website . . . where parents can sign up to receive email or text message alerts from me,"[71] says Terre Haute, Indiana, teacher Marie Williams Wimsett.

Textbooks and Flexbooks

As high schools and colleges move further toward cyber-based education, textbooks may also undergo radical changes. Many textbook publishers are offering online versions of their printed books, which students can download onto their laptops or e-readers. Some of these textbooks are known as "flexbooks," meaning the teachers can alter the content to more closely follow the material covered in their courses or even to make the subject matter either more or less challenging to the students.

Flexbooks also enable the authors to change the text, updating them to keep their information current. Says Marc Aronson, an author of books for young readers, "When talking about meeting individual needs, we must remember that the printed textbook is not and never was really a book. It's merely an instructional device that offers materials that make it easier for the teacher to plan and the student to learn. . . . Think of a textbook as an atlas or dictionary—a supplement for a book. Once it's a digital book it can be used in more ways."[72]

Jacob Guggenheim, a 17-year-old high school student from Palo Alto, California, says he has used e-books and prefers them over printed texts. "They're fun to work with," he says. "There are search functions to [help you] pick out a particular chapter. . . . I'm prone to losing textbooks, so that's $75 down the drain."[73]

> "What we're finding is that students are not that comfortable with electronic media. They still like the idea of holding and feeling a book."[75]
>
> — Stacy Volnick, director of business services for Florida Atlantic University.

Many school administrators believe it makes economic sense to use e-books. In recent years many e-book readers have come down in price and can be purchased for about $100. Certainly, that is more than the cost of the average textbook, but most e-readers can hold hundreds or even thousands of titles. In California, a statewide project to substitute e-books for bound textbooks is expected to save some $300 million a year.

Taking Phys Ed . . . Online

With her schedule loaded with advanced placement classes, Boca Raton, Florida, high school student Lynda Figueredo had no time to take physical education—even though she needed the class to graduate. And so she elected to take PE—online. She says, "At first, I thought, 'Online PE? That's kind of weird."

Nevertheless, Figueredo is one of about 1,700 Florida high school students who enrolled in an online PE class. As part of the class, students learn exercise techniques and health information. They must also exercise regularly and keep logs of progress as well as their eating habits. Online PE students also learn how to monitor their heart rates, and they report that information to the teacher as well.

While the system appears ripe for abuse, online PE teacher Jo Wagner says most students take the class seriously and do their homework—meaning they exercise. Also, Wagner says, she stays in contact with the students' parents. "The parents are very honest about whether their kids have been working out," says Wagner. "It's actually been a neat way to see families connect or reconnect around a common goal of fitness and nutrition."

Quoted in Scott Travis, "Some High Schoolers Take Physical Education—by Computer," *South Florida Sun-Sentinel*, July 17, 2003.

Former governor Arnold Schwarzenegger, a proponent of the conversion to e-books before he left office in 2011, also points out the environmental advantages of e-books, which do not require the destruction of trees to make paper. "Number one, you don't have to carry around this heavy load in your bag, in your school bag, which my kids always complain about," he says. "And number two, I think it will help because you don't have to cut down as many trees. Think about that, how much paper is being used in those textbooks."[74]

Some educators are not ready to endorse e-books. By 2011 many e-book readers did not permit users to underline, highlight, bookmark, or otherwise add notes to what they are reading. (While public high school students are usually not permitted to highlight text or otherwise make notations in textbooks, that is routine practice for college students who typically buy their books.) Until the technology catches up with the way students read textbooks, some educators believe students are better off with printed textbooks. "What we're finding is that students are not that comfortable with electronic media," says Stacy Volnick, director of business services for Florida Atlantic University. "They still like the idea of holding and feeling a book."[75]

Detecting Plagiarism

Another advantage to text delivered digitally is that it can usually be cut and pasted into students' assignments without the need for a lot of retyping. That could be a time-saver for many students—as long as they follow the rules and cite the sources for the copied materials. Unfortunately, some students do not follow the rules; they commit plagiarism—the theft of written text which they claim as their own work. Some plagiarists cut and paste passages drawn from other sources, while others download entire term papers that are available for sale online.

What plagiarists do not realize, though, is that plagiarism is often easy to detect. Most teachers are well aware of the intellectual abilities of their students, and when those students turn in term papers that appear to be far more scholarly than what they have received from those students in the past, warning bells are sure to chime.

> "What really makes us intelligent isn't our ability to find lots of information quickly. It's our ability to think deeply about that information."[79]
>
> — Author Nicholas Carr.

Susan Maximon, a social studies teacher at Fairview High School in Boulder, Colorado, is among the many teachers who have read term papers that seemed beyond the intellectual capabilities of their students. In one case, Maximon recalls reading a term paper turned in by an eleventh-grade student and concluding very early on that the student was not the author. "I knew he didn't write it," she says. "It was filled with big words and expressions that he never used and probably didn't understand."[76]

Moreover, software has been developed that helps teachers identify plagiarism. These programs rely on keywords found in the text, which

Improved e-reader technology has led to a boom in e-book use. Many publishers, schools, and libraries are investing in e-books but some educators say they still prefer that their students use printed books.

are then compared to words found in documents stored in Internet databases. Says John Barrie, president of an Oakland, California, company that designs software that helps sniff out plagiarized work,

> There's a belief among young people that materials found online are free, or are somehow inherently different from something you buy at a record store or get out of a book or magazine. Kids download music from the Internet even though it's a form of intellectual-property theft. It's naïve to think that attitude is not going to have a large impact on plagiarism at educational institutions.[77]

Is Google Harmful to Education?

Students who plagiarize can find a ready accomplice on the Internet that helps them find term papers to download. That accomplice is Google or a similar search engine.

E-books and Textbooks: By the Numbers

The average e-book costs between $10 and $15, making it far less expensive than the average textbook, which could cost $50 or more. At that cost per book, according to the College Board, which studies trends at American universities, most university students would see substantial savings over what they spend a year on textbooks. That cost, the College Board says, currently totals more than $1,100 a year.

The typical e-reader weighs just a few ounces and can hold hundreds or even thousands of titles. In contrast, to find some textbooks weighing in at seven pounds or more is not unusual. In 2010 *Information Today* magazine estimated that the typical e-reader can hold four tons worth of books—or roughly the weight of an African elephant.

Some educational authorities have become so concerned about the weight of textbooks—and how they may cause back injuries to students who tote them around in backpacks—that they have told publishers to make them lighter. In 2004, for example, the California Department of Education capped the weight of high school textbooks at five pounds.

Honest students use Google as well—always with the best intentions, as they hope the search engine will help them find information for the topics they are researching. And Google unquestionably can help—after all, the motto of the company is, "To organize the world's information and make it universally accessible and useful."[78]

Some experts question whether using Google or another search engine is truly the best strategy for researching a term paper or other project. By making research so easy, they ask, have search engines caused people to be less intuitive? Do people let Google do much of the work for them, then accept results that may be close to what they seek—but not ideal? "I worry about what Google is doing to our brains," says Nicholas Carr, who has explored the impact of the Internet on intellectualism.

What really makes us intelligent isn't our ability to find lots of information quickly. It's our ability to think deeply about that information. And deep thinking, brain scientists have discovered, happens only when our minds are calm and attentive. The greater our concentration, the richer our thoughts. . . . The fact is, you never think deeply if you're always Googling, texting, and surfing.[79]

Some educators agree. David Ellis, a professor at York University in Toronto, Canada, says,

Google isn't making us stupid—but it is making many of us intellectually lazy. This has already become a big problem in university classrooms. For my undergrad majors in Communication Studies, Google may take over the hard work involved in finding good source material for written assignments. Unless pushed in the right direction, students will opt for the top 10 or 15 hits as their research strategy. . . . Stronger intellects will use Google as a creative tool, while others will let Google do the thinking for them.[80]

But Google has its defenders who argue that the search engine is a tool that has opened up tremendous quantities of information to people who would not otherwise have access to that information. Says Peter Norvig, director of research for Google, "Just as a car allows us to move faster and a telescope lets us see farther, access to the Internet's information lets us think better and faster. By considering a wide range of information, we can arrive at more creative and informed solutions. Internet users are more likely to be exposed to a diversity of ideas."[81]

> "Just as a car allows us to move faster and a telescope lets us see farther, access to the Internet's information lets us think better and faster."[81]
>
> — Peter Norvig, director of research for Google.

Treasure Trove of Information

Norvig and other advocates for using Google and other search engines point out that the technology behind search is bound to improve in the future—meaning that searching the Internet may become much more fulfilling for some people than it may be now. Certainly, as the Internet becomes a bigger part of people's lives, schools and colleges will continue to look for ways to tap its resources to enhance the education of students.

Online classes may become more common. Electronic versions of textbooks and other books may be used more frequently in classrooms. Many students will react positively to these trends, while some will likely find ways to skip assignments, plagiarize term papers, and find other ways to abuse the vast treasure trove of information available online.

Chapter Five

The Future of Online Information and Research

Researchers at the University of Iowa believe they have found a way to track influenza outbreaks: They study Google searches that have used keywords describing flu symptoms. By working with engineers at Google, the Iowa researchers can tell in what parts of the country the searches originate and the type of flu symptoms for which most people appear to be seeking information. "This could conceivably provide as early a warning of an outbreak as any system," says Lyn Finelli, a staff member in the influenza division of the Centers for Disease Control and Prevention. "The earlier the warning, the earlier prevention and control measures can be put in place, and this could prevent cases of influenza."[82]

Google's philanthropic division, Google.org, assisted the Iowa researchers by providing the data and developing a web-searching tool, Google Flu Trends, that assists in collating the data. The flu detection program is still considered experimental; by 2011, no public health agency was using it to track flu outbreaks. Still, the development of Google Flu Trends illustrates how searching the Internet is a dynamic science. Because of newly discovered ways information can be accessed through Internet searching, the way people travel, shop, enjoy their leisure time, and even avoid illnesses may be far different in a few years than it is now.

Searching the Invisible Web

As search engines continue to refine their capabilities, they will likely become able to probe more of the Internet than they are currently able to

People searching online for information about influenza symptoms may provide a means for researchers to track flu epidemics. This research could lead to an early warning system that might prevent major epidemics such as the one that began in Mexico (pictured) in 2009.

do. As difficult as it may be to imagine, most search engines are actually only skimming the surface of what is available online.

Many experts believe a small fraction of the Internet is accessed through common searches. Because they are based on links and page views, most Internet searches skip sites that either lack links or much user traffic. This region of the Internet is known as the "Deep Web" or "Invisible Web," and it is believed to contain abundant information that could be useful to students and other researchers. Data that can be mined from the Invisible Web include job listings, information on stocks and other investments, addresses and telephone numbers, airline flight information, reports by government agencies, and an abundance of statistical data that is not usually available through common searches.

As Internet use moves into the future, engineers are expected to develop software and searching techniques that will provide access to the Invisible Web. Write authors Chris Sherman and Gary Price, experts on accessing the Invisible Web, "The Invisible Web holds incredibly valuable resources for the researcher. Journeys into the Invisible Web lead not only to treasures that aren't easily located, but often provide the pleasures and satisfaction experienced by early explorers who led expeditions into regions of the world marked *Terra Incognito* on early maps."[83]

Finding First-Rate Information

Invisible Web search engines will start with keywords to see what type of information they produce. Then, the search engines of the future will automatically insert additional keywords, continually honing the results until they develop a profile of the information contained on the invisible sites. In other words, the Invisible Web engine will provide very specific information on Internet pages that do not ordinarily lend themselves to keyword searches.

A major hurdle for researchers will be how to find these keywords in places where most search engines do not ordinarily look for them—such as court records and scientific documents. "The crawlable Web is the tip of the iceberg," says Anand Rajaraman, cofounder of Kosmix, a company developing an Invisible Web search engine. "Most search engines try to help you find a needle in a haystack but what we're trying to do is help you explore the haystack."[84]

> "The crawlable Web is the tip of the iceberg. Most search engines try to help you find a needle in a haystack but what we're trying to do is help you explore the haystack."[84]
>
> — Anand Rajaraman, cofounder of Kosmix, a company developing an Invisible Web search engine.

Early results from experimental Invisible Web search engines have shown their abilities to access and categorize up to 90 percent of the information stored in databases that otherwise would not turn up in Google or Bing searches. Says Chris Sherman, the associate editor of SearchEngineWatch.com, "We are not talking about information of dubious value, such as spam . . . or Uncle Edwin's trout fishing gallery. A big chunk of the Invisible Web consists of first-rate information maintained by reputable, authoritative sources—treasure troves for the users that can find it."[85]

Probing the Invisible Web Today

Actually, Internet users do not have to wait for the development of search engines that can probe the Invisible Web. Some techniques are already available to uncover information in the Invisible Web. Joseph W. Barker, former reference librarian at the University of California at Berkeley, says searches using Google and Bing can uncover information in the Invisible Web if one of the keywords employed in the search is "database." He says, "Simply think 'databases' and keep your eyes open. You can find searchable databases containing Invisible Web pages in the course of routine searching in most general Web directories."[86]

As an example, Barker uses the term "plane crash database." A simple Google search using those keywords uncovers a database maintained by the National Transportation Safety Board that enables users to search for details on specific crashes or to trawl through chronological lists of accidents. Confining the Google search to the keywords "plane crash," without using the word "database" in the search, would likely turn up thousands of organic results on various plane crashes that have occurred over a large span of time. By employing the term "database" in the search, the user has a better chance of locating the specific plane crash for which he or she seeks information.

> "We can't pretend people will go back to walking into a library and talking to a reference librarian. We have to respond to these new ways."[88]
>
> — Kate Wittenberg, director of the Electronic Publishing Initiative at Columbia University in New York.

Abundance of E-Books

Even as software engineers develop the technology to probe the Invisible Web, the searchable web available to most users today continues to grow. One area in which the web is exploding with information concerns digitized books available to be read online or as downloads. According to

Digitizing the Vatican Library

The Vatican Library houses some of the oldest printed materials in existence. Some of the library's documents are more than 1,000 years old. One such document is the *Historia Arcana*, which scholars have determined is an encyclopedia written by a Byzantine author, Procopius, in the tenth century. To view the *Historia Arcana* as well as other documents, scholars have always had to travel to the Vatican in Rome, Italy.

That situation is changing, though, thanks to the decision by the Vatican to digitize its collection, making the library's contents available on the Internet. The project is expected to take until 2020. Once the scanning of the materials is completed, scholars will have online access to nearly 2 million books, manuscripts, and other documents—some many hundreds of years old.

Because of the delicacy of the documents, only professional scholars are granted permission to review them in the library's reading rooms. After the documents are scanned, though, anybody with Internet access can inspect them. "The library is open to the general public over the website," says Didier Philippe, director of corporate development for Hewlett-Packard, the American technology company assisting the Vatican in the digitization of its library. "You can now see things such as a manuscript from Michelangelo, and there will be more information and images available online as time goes on."

Quoted in Laura Rohde, "Ancient Manuscripts Go Online," *PC World*, October 29, 2002. www.pcworld.com.

the trade organization Book Industry Study Group, e-books grew from representing 1.5 percent of the publishing market in 2009 to 5 percent in 2010. Readers can find these books at Amazon.com and similar retailers or through their public libraries.

Digital versions of books—as well as newspapers and magazines—can also be found in online databases, such as EBSCO Host, InfoTrac, LexisNexis and ProQuest. These are typically fee based, although many public libraries offer them free to cardholders, and school libraries may make them available to students. Others are free, such as Project Gutenberg, a nonprofit organization that offers thousands of free e-book downloads.

Generally, the copyrights on books available on these sites have expired, meaning they are available in the public domain. When copyrights expire, publishers as well as authors and their heirs cease collecting royalties on book sales. Therefore, the books are free for downloading by anybody.

Controversy over Google Books

Google is also underwriting a long-term project to digitize books. The company has estimated that currently, nearly 130 million titles are available worldwide and that its intentions are to digitize all of them. Moreover, using the tools available on Google Books, users can enter keywords to find specific passages or other information.

Google commenced scanning books in 2004 and by late 2010 announced that it had scanned some 15 million titles. Said James Crawford, director of engineering for Google Books, "The greater the diversity of content on the Web, the more useful it becomes. And the more people who can access the information cataloged in books, the more enlightening those works become."[87]

Unlike Project Gutenberg, the project by Google Books involves many editions that have current copyrights, meaning that the authors and publishers are still collecting royalties on the books. The project has created major friction between Google and many of America's authors and book publishers. They contend that making those books available free online violates the copyrights and deprives authors and publishers of the money they would receive from people who would buy the books if they could not find them online for free.

> "[Readers] want to participate, make comments, interact with other readers, and somehow take ownership of the content."[90]
>
> — Thomas Frey, executive director at the futurist think tank DeVinci Institute.

Google responded to the complaints by insisting that it had "fair use" to the books, a provision under US copyright law that permits students, researchers, and others to use portions of copyrighted material without compensating the copyright holder. Moreover, Google pointed out, to comply with fair use provisions it does not scan every page of books with current copyrights but leaves many of those pages missing. Publishers as well as groups representing authors were not satisfied with that explanation and have filed several lawsuits against Google claiming copyright infringement. Google attempted to reach a settlement with many of those cases by establishing a $125 million fund to compensate copyright holders when their books are made available on Google Books. In 2011, though, a federal judge rejected Google's offer to settle the cases, finding that creation of the fund still does not satisfy copyright law. The judge pointed out that Google does not seek permission from the copyright holders before digitizing the books, but merely offers to compensate them after the books are digitized. As the case moves forward, legal experts suggest, Google may be forced to reach agreements for compensation with publishers and authors prior to scanning their books.

> "Books will last because they fulfill some basic human needs, not only in what they convey but how they convey, how they feel, and how they fit into our lives."[92]
>
> — Barry Fast, board member of the International Library and Analytical Center.

Libraries of the Future

As more books become available on the web, libraries face the challenge of how to stay relevant in a world of digital information. Many libraries have responded by taking steps to digitize their collections, making their books and other materials available online. Says Kate Wittenberg, director of the Electronic Publishing Initiative at Columbia University in New York, "We can't pretend people will go back to walking into a library and talking to a reference librarian. We have to respond to these new ways."[88]

In fact, the library of the future is likely to bear little resemblance to the classic notion of a library—a building featuring shelves and shelves of books. Libraries see themselves as becoming digital media centers: places where readers can access and read e-books as well as other digitized media, including videos and video games. Libraries know they can no longer be places providing a "one-way flow of information,"[89] according to Thomas Frey, executive director at the futurist think tank DeVinci Institute. In other words, he says, libraries can no longer just be places where people go to borrow books. "[Readers] want to participate, make comments, interact with other readers, and somehow take ownership of the content," says Frey. "The possibilities are endless. Some will offer a selection of digital tablets and book readers, others will feature mini-theaters, gamer stations, day-care centers [and] working studios."[90]

Frey believes the future library may not even feature books. He says,

> During the coming years, libraries will be faced with a number of options for replacing their current inventory of books with electronic book readers. As some . . . libraries begin to understand the economics and freedoms [and] restrictions associated with the devices, they will begin to move forward, replacing thousands of volumes on the rack with what will seem like a relatively few e-readers occupying comparatively little space.[91]

Still, many librarians and other experts insist that printed books will remain on library shelves for many years to come. "Books will last because they fulfill some basic human needs, not only in what they convey but how they convey, how they feel, and how they fit into our lives," says Barry Fast, a board member of the International Library and Analytical Center, which studies issues involving American libraries. "Like the wheel—with us from prehistoric times—books carry us from here to there, and like the Internet, they carry us sometimes with awe and mystery."[92]

Learning Search Commands

As libraries change, librarians are finding themselves taking on new responsibilities. School librarians, in particular, are becoming experts in accessing online data. "School librarians are needed more than ever now to deal with changes in the instructional environment,"[93] says Ann M. Martin, a former president of the American Association of School Libraries (AASL).

For example, librarians are mastering the use of search commands, which help students and others narrow their searches. Google estimates

Some predict the library of the future will be a digital media center rather than a traditional building filled with shelves of books, but many librarians and other experts believe that printed books will continue to circulate in libraries for years to come.

that search commands are used on less than 5 percent of its searches, but if people become more familiar with search commands they can cut through a lot of the dross that turns up on their organic search pages.

Search commands include putting quotation marks around keywords so that Google can find exact phrases; using the minus sign to exclude certain words, and the asterisk to use as a placeholder for unknown words. For example, if a researcher wants to know how a certain senator voted on certain bills but is not sure which bills to include in the search, the asterisk will ask the search engine to fill in the blanks. The keywords in such a search may appear as: Senator Smith voted * on the * bill. "You can just Google it, and you can be hip-deep in it or armpit-deep in it," says Julie Walker, executive director of the AASL. "But that doesn't mean you have the information that meets your needs."[94]

Making Search More Meaningful

A major development in searching the Internet is expected to focus on making searches more meaningful to the searchers. Search engine designers readily admit that most searches do not give the user exactly what he or she wants. To improve searching, the user's computer and the search engine have to do a better job of understanding the searcher's needs.

Therefore, individual computers will be programmed to learn the habits of the user, developing a profile of the user. Today, somebody using a search engine to shop for clothes will likely be led to a number of online retailers. From there, the searcher will enter data—size, price, color, style, and so on—and then cull through the results until the shopper ultimately finds what he or she is looking for if, indeed, the search is successful.

In the future, the computer will already know the size of the user, the prices the user prefers to pay for clothes, and the style of clothes the user prefers. The user will still be led to a list of retailers, but the list will be refined and more specific, giving the user better choices. "For clothes, you want sizes and colors—and perhaps some filters depending on your personal characteristics,"[95] says Esther Dyson, head of an e-commerce investments company.

Retailers like Amazon.com already try to develop something of a profile of users based on their past shopping habits. A user who has pur-

Library 2.0

Traditionally, a library is a place where people go to find information—often in books. The people who decide which books to obtain for the libraries are usually librarians.

That operational model is expected to change as libraries adopt the principles of a movement known as "Library 2.0." Under this concept, cardholders play a role in deciding which materials the library provides. "The heart of Library 2.0 is user-centered change," reports the *Library Journal*. "It is a model for library service . . . inviting user participation in the creation of both the physical and the virtual services they want."

Librarians who have adopted Library 2.0 principles have created blogs, Facebook pages, or Twitter accounts to enhance communications with cardholders. Other libraries have taken the concept a step further by inviting cardholders to actually create the content that will be archived at the library. At the Public Library of Charlotte and Mecklenburg County in North Carolina, librarians have set up multimedia rooms for young members, inviting them to record music or make videos. Said Kelly Czarnecki, technology education librarian, "Our motto here is to bring stories to life, so by having the movie and music studio we can really tap into a different angle of what stories are. They're not just in books. They're something kids can create themselves."

Michael E. Casey and Laura C. Savastinuk, "Library 2.0," *Library Journal*, September 1, 2006. www.libraryjournal.com.

Quoted in John D. Sutter, "The Future of Libraries, with or Without Books," CNN, September 4, 2009. http://articles.cnn.com.

chased a book written by a particular author may receive an e-mail from the online bookseller notifying him or her when another book by that author has been published. Also, Amazon.com notifies users that others who have ordered the same book also ordered other, specific titles. The rationale at work here is that people who read the same books often have similar interests and may be willing to buy similar books.

The Arrival of Semantic Searching

Another new phase for Internet searching will be so-called "semantic searching." Today, the typical search is initiated by entering an average of three keywords into the search bar. From those three words, a searcher hopes to find answers to what could be some very complex questions. Why not put the question directly to Google or another search engine in, well, the form of a question?

Right now, searchers can type questions into the search bars but Google and the other search engines do not specifically respond to the questions, they pick out keywords in the questions and respond to those. In the near future, as the software for semantic searching becomes more refined, it may be possible to pose an actual question in the search bar and be rewarded with a list of websites that contain the specific answer. And as semantic searching becomes more of a reality, speech recognition software is expected to develop as well. Therefore, in a few years, simply verbalizing the question may be possible. The computer will pick up the user's voice and respond by searching the web for the answer.

For searchers who want to narrow their queries to people and sources they trust, the use of a system known as Aardvark may become more common. People who intend to travel may be searching for a good hotel, airline, or other service. Aardvark looks at the user's e-mail lists, Facebook friends, and similar sources, then culls through blogs, Twitter messages, and other material from those contacts seeking answers to the query. A friend may have blogged about a good experience in a particular hotel—this is the type of information that Aardvark would help uncover.

> "You can just Google it, and you can be hip-deep in it or armpit-deep in it, but that doesn't mean you have the information that meets your needs."[94]
>
> — Julie Walker, executive director of the American Association of School Librarians.

Information: A Vital Part of Life

A wealth of information is available on the Internet. The development of search engines capable of probing the Invisible Web will open up even greater troves of data to searchers. Moreover, the development of semantic search software could make information much easier to find. And the further development of computers could mean that the machines will be able to tell what type of information the user seeks without the user having to spell out desires in the form of specific keywords.

Given the great strides in technology and the promise of what lies ahead, it is often difficult to remember that the Internet has only been around since 1969. In the four decades since the operators of those two university computers in California made very brief contact with one another, the Internet has truly grown into an information superhighway. The Internet's ability to provide information to people has become not only a vital component of their lives, but a component they would be hard-pressed to live without.

Source Notes

Introduction: All the World's Information

1. Quoted in Jill Smolowe, Nicole Weisensee Egan, and Diane Herbst, "Found After 23 Years," *People*, February 7, 2011, p. 50.
2. Quoted in Smolowe, Egan, and Herbst, "Found After 23 Years," p. 50.
3. Nicholas Carr, "Is Google Making Us Stupid?," *Atlantic*, July/August 2008. www.theatlantic.com.
4. John Battelle, *The Search: How Google and Its Rivals Rewrote the Rules of Business and Transformed Our Culture*. New York: Penguin, 2005, pp. 12–13.

Chapter One: Evolution of the Information Superhighway

5. Quoted in Denise R. Superville, "Hours Spent Wired Changing How Kids Think and Interact," *Hackensack Record*, June 1, 2010.
6. Quoted in Superville, "Hours Spent Wired Changing How Kids Think and Interact."
7. Quoted in Ken Auletta, "Searching for Trouble," *New Yorker*, October 12, 2009, p. 56.
8. Quoted in Candace Lombardi, "Google Joins Xerox as a Verb," July 6, 2006, CNET News. http://news.cnet.com.
9. Quoted in Christine Frey and John Cook, "How Amazon.com Survived, Thrived, and Turned a Profit," *Seattle Post-Intelligencer*, January 28, 2004. www.seattlepi.com.
10. Battelle, *The Search*, p. 39.
11. Ken Auletta, *Googled: The End of the World as We Know It*. New York: Penguin, 2009, p. 38.
12. Aaron Goldman, *Everything I Know About Marketing I Learned from Google*. New York: McGraw Hill, 2011, p. 27.
13. Quoted in Michael Specter, "Search and Deploy," *New Yorker*, May 29, 2000, p. 88.
14. Quoted in Specter, "Search and Deploy," p. 88.
15. Deborah Fallows, *Search Engine Users*. Washington, DC: Pew Internet & American Life Project, 2005, p. i.

16. Deborah Fallows, "Search Soars, Challenging Email as a Favorite Internet Activity," Pew Research Center, August 6, 2008. http://pew research.org.

17. Quoted in CNN, "Experts: Information Onslaught Bad for Your Health," April 15, 1997. www.cnn.com.

18. Ann Blair, "Information Overload, Then and Now," *Chronicle of Higher Education*, December 3, 2010, p. B4.

19. Andrew Kantor, "Internet Suffering from Information Overload," *USA Today*, June 14, 2007. www.usatoday.com.

20. Kantor, "Internet Suffering from Information Overload."

21. Kantor, "Internet Suffering from Information Overload."

22. Greg R. Notess, *Teaching Web Search Skills: Techniques and Strategies of Top Trainers*. Medford, NJ: Information Today, 2007, pp. 8–9.

23. Notess, *Teaching Web Search Skills*, p. 76.

24. Quoted in Notess, *Teaching Web Search Skills*, p. 75.

Chapter Two: How Reliable Is Information Found Online?

25. Quoted in John Seigenthaler Sr., "A False Wikipedia 'Biography,'" *USA Today*, November 29, 2005. www.usatoday.com.

26. Seigenthaler, "A False Wikipedia 'Biography.'"

27. Robert Harris, "Evaluating Internet Research Sources," November 22, 2010. www.virtualsalt.com.

28. Harris, "Evaluating Internet Research Sources."

29. Wendy Boswell, *The About.com Guide to Online Research*. Avon, MA: Adams Media, 2007, p. 151.

30. Quoted in Brock Read, "Can Wikipedia Ever Make the Grade?," *Chronicle of Higher Education*, October 27, 2006, p. 31.

31. Quoted in Stacy Schiff, "Know It All," *New Yorker*, July 31, 2006, p. 36.

32. Quoted in Helen Leggatt, "Local Newspaper Websites Most Trusted Online," BizReport, February 26, 2010. www.bizreport.com.

33. Bill Gates, "Support Freedom of Expression on the Internet," February 22, 1996. http://scripting.com.

34. Boswell, *The About.com Guide to Online Research*, pp. 183–84.

35. Dave Warlick, *Classroom Blogging: Teacher's Guide to Blogs, Wikis, and Other Tools That Are Shaping a New Information Landscape*. Raleigh, NC: Landmark, 2007, p. 39.

36. Quoted in Dick Meyer, "Blogging as Typing, Not Journalism," CBS News, November 8, 2004. www.cbsnews.com.

37. Quoted in *PBS NewsHour*, "Weblogging," April 28, 2003. www.pbs. org.

38. Quoted in *PBS NewsHour*, "Weblogging."

39. 100bestwebsites.org, "The 100 Best Websites List," 2010. www.100 bestwebsites.org.

Chapter Three: The Business of Search and Information

40. Goldman, *Everything I Know About Marketing I Learned from Google*, p. 92.

41. Goldman, *Everything I Know About Marketing I Learned from Google*, p. 92.

42. Goldman, *Everything I Know About Marketing I Learned from Google*, p. 57.

43. Quoted in Lucy Handley, "Maximize Your Search Appeal," *Marketing Week*, December 2, 2010, p. 24.

44. Quoted in Handley, "Maximize Your Search Appeal," p. 24.

45. Goldman, *Everything I Know About Marketing I Learned from Google*, p. 221.

46. Robert L. Dilenschneider, *The AMA Handbook of Public Relations: Leveraging PR in the Digital World*. New York: Amacom, 2010, p. 19.

47. Dilenschneider, *The AMA Handbook of Public Relations*, p. 14.

48. Quoted in CNN, "Murdoch: Websites to Charge for Content," May 7, 2009. www.cnn.com.

49. Quoted in CNN, "Murdoch: Websites to Charge for Content."

50. Quoted in Joseph Tartakoff, "Taking the Plunge: How Newspaper Sites That Charge Are Faring," PaidContent.org, September 2, 2009. http://paidcontent.org.

51. Keith Whistler, "Net Neutrality Is Necessary," Save the Internet, August 5, 2010. www.savetheinternet.com.

52. Al Franken, "Net Neutrality, Comcast-NBC Deal Threaten the Web," January 21, 2011. http://blog.alfranken.com.

53. Kay Bailey Hutchinson, "Unnecessary Intervention," *USA Today*, January 4, 2011, p. 6A.

54. Quoted in Eitb.com, "Spanish Telefónica to Charge Google, Yahoo, Bing," February 6, 2010. www.eitb.com.

55. Quoted in Stanley Pignal, "Telecom Groups Warned on Data Charges," *Financial Times*, April 14, 2010, p. 6.

56. Quoted in Pignal, "Telecom Groups Warned on Data Charges," p. 6.

Chapter Four: How Is Online Information Changing the Classroom?

57. Quoted in Marc Parry, "Tomorrow's College," *Chronicle of Higher Education*, November 5, 2010, p. B4.

58. Quoted in Parry, "Tomorrow's College," p. B4.

59. Quoted in Tim Engle, "Virtual Students Go to School Without Being in School," McClatchy Newspapers, October 18, 2009.

60. Quoted in Mark Rowh, "E-learning: The Anytime, Anywhere Option," *Career World*, October 2007, p. 22.

61. Quoted in Rowh, "E-learning," p. 22.

62. Quoted in Engle, "Virtual Students Go to School Without Being in School."

63. Quoted in Parry, "Tomorrow's College," p. B4.

64. Quoted in Engle, "Virtual Students Go to School Without Being in School."

65. Quoted in Engle, "Virtual Students Go to School Without Being in School."

66. Quoted in Rowh, "E-learning," p. 22.

67. Quoted in Engle, "Virtual Students Go to School Without Being in School."

68. I. Elaine Allen and Jeff Seaman, *Class Differences: Online Education in the United States, 2010*. Boston: US Distance Learning Association, November 2010. www.usdla.org.

69. Margie Martyn, "The Hybrid Online Model: Good Practice," *Educause Quarterly*, 2003, p. 19.

70. Lemoyne S. Dunn, "Making the Most of Your Class Website," *Educational Leadership*, February 2011, p. 60.

71. Quoted in *Scholastic Instructor*, "Teachers Weigh In," 2010, p. 14.

72. Quoted in Rebecca Hill, "Turning the Page," *School Library Journal*, October 2010, p. 24.

73. Quoted in *Junior Scholastic*, "Digital Textbooks in Schools?," September 21, 2009, p. 4.

74. Quoted in *Current Events*, "Textbook Toss-Up," September 7, 2009, p. 7.

75. Quoted in Scott Travis, "Are Textbooks Becoming Obsolete? As E-books Evolve, Students Who Are Partial to Print Might Choose Digital Versions," *Fort Lauderdale Sun-Sentinel*, July 7, 2009, p. A1.

76. Quoted in Brian Hansen, "Combating Plagiarism," *CQ Researcher*, September 19, 2003, p. 773.

77. Quoted in Hansen, "Combating Plagiarism," p. 773.

78. Google, "Google's Mission Is to Organize the World's Information and Make It Universally Accessible and Useful," Google Corporate Information, 2011. www.google.com.

79. Nicholas Carr, "Is Google Making Us Stupid? Yes," *New York Times Upfront*, October 4, 2010, p. 22.

80. Quoted in Janna Quitney Anderson and Lee Raine, "Does Google Make Us Stupid?," Pew Research Center, February 19, 2010. http://pewresearch.org.

81. Peter Norvig, "Is Google Making Us Stupid? No," *New York Times Upfront*, October 4, 2010, p. 22.

Chapter Five: The Future of Online Information and Research

82. Quoted in Miguel Helft, "Using the Internet to Track Flu's Spread," *New York Times*, November 11, 2009. www.nytimes.com.

83. Chris Sherman and Gary Price, *The Invisible Web: Uncovering Information Sources Search Engines Can't Reach*. Medford, NJ: Today, 2007, p. xxvii.

84. Quoted in Alex Wright, "Exploring a 'Deep Web' That Google Can't Grasp," *New York Times*, February 23, 2009, p. B4.

85. Chris Sherman, "Online: Search for the Invisible Web," *London Guardian*, September 6, 2001, p. 1.

86. Joseph W. Barker, "Invisible or Deep Web: What It Is, How to Find It, and Its Inherent Ambiguity," January 2004. www.lib.berkeley.edu.

87. James Crawford, "On the Future of Books," Inside Google Books, October 14, 2010. http://booksearch.blogspot.com.

88. Quoted in Katie Hafner, "Old Search Engine, the Library, Tries to Fit into a Google World," *New York Times*, June 21, 2004, p. A1.

89. Quoted in *American Libraries*, "The Future of Libraries: Interview with Thomas Frey," July 16, 2010. http://americanlibrariesmagazine.org.
90. Quoted in *American Libraries*, "The Future of Libraries: Interview with Thomas Frey."
91. Thomas Frey, "Where the Books Used to Be," December 10, 2010. www.futuristspeaker.com.
92. Quoted in Paul E. Howard and Renee Y. Rastorfer, "Do We Still Need Books?," *Law Library Journal*, Spring 2005, p. 258.
93. Quoted in Lawrence Hardy, "The Future of School Libraries," *American School Board Journal*, January 2010, p. 23.
94. Quoted in Hardy, "The Future of School Libraries," p. 24.
95. Esther Dyson, "The Future of Internet Search," Project Syndicate, August 19, 2010. www.project-syndicate.org.

Facts About Online Information and Research

- Amazon.com reported in 2010 that its sales of e-books surpassed those of hardbacks by a margin of 143 e-books to every 100 hardbacks; a year later, the online retailer reported e-books had outsold paperbacks by a margin of 115 to 100.

- A 2010 study by the Pew Internet & American Life Project reported that 63 percent of American teenagers spend at least part of every day online.

- Hitwise, a service that analyzes Internet use, reported in 2011 that 82 percent of Bing users are satisfied with the results they receive from the search engine; meanwhile, 65 percent of Google users say they are satisfied with their search results.

- A 2010 study underwritten by the Pew Project for Excellence in Journalism found that just 43 percent of the 60 most highly regarded news-oriented blogs are updated with fresh material at least once a day.

- A 2008 poll by the Gallup Organization found that 31 percent of respondents receive their news directly from the Internet; a similar poll taken in 2006 reported that just 22 percent of respondents obtain their news from the Internet.

- A 2008 poll by Zogby International reported that 37 percent of respondents found the Internet the most reliable source of news, while 20 percent found network TV broadcasts the most reliable, and 16 percent said radio broadcasts are most reliable.

- Internet marketing expert Aaron Goldman reports in his 2011 book *Everything I Know About Marketing I Learned from Google* that the keywords "car insurance" and "auto insurance" are entered in the Google search bar an average of 38 million times a month.

- A 2010 survey by the Rasmussen Poll found that 52 percent of respondents believe the Federal Communications Commission should not regulate Internet content.

- Three hundred members of the US House and Senate signed a letter in 2010 opposing net neutrality.

- A 2010 study by JISC Collections, a British academic research company, reported that 85 percent of students spend less than one minute reading an e-book page and that just 5.5 percent of students read the whole book.

- A 2010 study by the Pew Internet & American Life Project found that of nearly 400 educators polled, 81 percent believe the use of Google makes people smarter, while 16 percent believe using Google will make people less intelligent.

- Public Interest Research Group, a consumer rights organization, reported the results of a study in 2009 that found 75 percent of college students prefer using printed textbooks rather than e-books.

- McClatchy Newspapers reported in 2009 that just 1 percent of students in American public schools are enrolled in online courses.

- In 2010 Southern New Hampshire University reported that its 50 online classes have drawn students from all 50 states as well as 22 foreign countries.

- A 2009 study by PBS reported that the Internet is used as an educational tool in 76 percent of American classrooms, from kindergarten through the twelfth grade.

- Forty-nine percent of teachers, school librarians, and other educators who responded to a 2011 poll by the George Lucas Educational Foundation said students should be permitted to use Wikipedia while researching term papers, while 36 percent said "maybe," 14 percent said "no," and 1 percent had no opinion.

- A 2009 study by the Pew Research Center for the People & the Press found 42 percent of respondents turn to the Internet as a source for national and international news, but just 17 percent find the Internet a valuable source for news about their hometowns.

- A 2008 study conducted by Harford Community College in Maryland judged Wikipedia articles to maintain an accuracy rate of 80 percent; entries in other sources, such as *Encyclopaedia Britannica* and the *Dictionary of American History,* were found to be accurate at least 95 percent of the time.

- A 2011 report by Domain Tools, a Seattle, Washington, company that tracks creation of Internet addresses, said that more than 155,000 new web pages are created every day; meanwhile, some 93,000 pages expire and are deleted from the web each day.

Related Organizations

American Library Association (ALA)

50 E. Huron St.
Chicago, IL 60611
phone: (800) 545-2433
fax: (312) 440-9374
e-mail: ala@ala.org
website: www.ala.org

The ALA is the professional association representing the nation's librarians. Visitors to the ALA website can find many resources about e-books and other Internet-based trends affecting American libraries. Several reports and updates on the ALA's program to encourage Library 2.0 initiatives in American libraries are also available.

Federal Communications Commission (FCC)

445 12th St. SW
Washington, DC 20554
phone: (888) 225-5322
fax: (866) 418-0232
e-mail: fccinfo@fcc.gov
website: www.fcc.gov

The Federal Communications Commission oversees regulations that affect electronic media in America, including the Internet. Students seeking information on net neutrality can find many resources on the agency's website, including statements in support of or opposition to net neutrality by the five FCC commissioners.

Google

1600 Amphitheatre Pkwy.
Mountain View, CA 94043
phone: (650) 253-0000
fax: (650) 253-0001
website: www.google.com

Students can find a lot of information about Google, the world's most popular search engine, by visiting the company's website. Students can learn about Google's history, its commitment to organizing the world's information, and the status of the company's many projects, including Google Books.

International Academy of Digital Arts and Sciences (IADAS)
19 West 21st St., Suite 602
New York, NY 10010
phone: (212) 675-4890
website: http://iadas.net

The academy serves as the trade association for professionals who design and administer websites. Each year, the academy sponsors the Webby Awards. The awards honor technical and artistic achievements but also recognize websites for the objectivity and accuracy of the information they provide.

National Newspaper Association (NNA)
120A E. Broad St.
Falls Church, VA 22046
phone: (800) 829-4662
fax: (703) 237-9808
website: www.nnaweb.org

The NNA represents the publishers of American newspapers. The organization has compiled many resources on how the Internet has affected American journalism. By entering "Internet" in the NNA website search engine, students can find more than 150 articles and reports that assess the value of online news.

Pew Internet & American Life Project
1615 L St. NW, Suite 700
Washington, DC 20036
phone: (202) 419-4500

fax: (202) 419-4505
e-mail: info@pewinternet.org
website: http://pewinternet.org

The Pew Internet & American Life Project studies how Americans use the Internet. Visitors to the organization's website can download copies of the report *Search Engine Users*, which describes how people use Google and other search engines and what sort of information they hope to obtain from their searches.

United States Distance Learning Association (USDLA)

8 Winter St., Suite 508
Boston, MA 02108
phone: (800) 275-5162
fax: (617) 399-1771
website: www.usdla.org

The USDLA promotes online learning at American colleges and high schools. Visitors to the organization's website can download copies of the USDLA's 2010 report *Class Differences: Online Education in the United States*, which contains many statistics on students who have enrolled in online college classes.

Wikimedia Foundation

149 New Montgomery St., 3rd Floor
San Francisco, CA 94105
phone: (415) 839-6885
fax: (415) 882-0495
e-mail: info@wikimedia.org
website: http://wikimediafoundation.org

Wikimedia Foundation is the nonprofit organization that administers the online encyclopedia Wikipedia. Visitors to the organization's website can find information on how Wikipedia is written as well as details on other projects, including the free online dictionary Wiktionary and a free source of e-books, Wikibooks.

For Further Research

Books

Ken Auletta, *Googled: The End of the World as We Know It*. New York: Penguin, 2009.

Jane Devine and Francine Egger-Sider, *Going Beyond Google: The Invisible Web in Learning and Teaching*. New York: Neal-Schuman, 2009.

Aaron Goldman, *Everything I Know About Marketing I Learned from Google*. New York: McGraw Hill, 2011.

Randolph Hock, *The Extreme Searcher's Internet Handbook: A Guide for the Serious Searcher*. Medford, NJ: Information Today, 2010.

Andrew Lih, *The Wikipedia Revolution: How a Bunch of Nobodies Created the World's Greatest Encyclopedia*. New York: Hyperion, 2009.

Periodicals

Ken Auletta, "Searching for Trouble," *New Yorker*, October 12, 2009.

Ann Blair, "Information Overload, Then and Now," *Chronicle of Higher Education*, December 3, 2010.

Nicholas Carr, "Is Google Making Us Stupid?," *Atlantic*, July/August 2008.

Rebecca Hill, "Turning the Page," *School Library Journal*, October 2010.

Alex Wright, "Exploring a 'Deep Web' That Google Can't Grasp," *New York Times*, February 23, 2009.

Internet Sources

Google, "Google Search Basics: More Search Help." www.google.com/support/websearch/bin/answer.py?hl=en&answer=136861.

Elizabeth E. Kirk, "Evaluating Information Found on the Internet," Sheridan Libraries, Johns Hopkins University, 1996. www.library.jhu.edu/researchhelp/general/evaluating.

MostPopularKeywords, "Fashion Keywords: Top Keywords for Search Engine Optimization (SEO) & Pay-Per-Click (PPC)," WordStream. www.wordstream.com/popular-keywords/fashion-keywords.

Dave Winer, "Bill Gates on Freedom," Scripting News, February 22, 1996. http://scripting.com/davenet/1996/02/22/billgatesonfreedom.html.

Websites

100 Best Websites (www.100bestwebsites.org). As the name suggests, 100 Best Websites lists the 100 websites that consistently deliver accurate and objective information. Organizers of the list include 23 criteria that determine the ratings for the sites. Each website is given a brief description as well as a link to the site.

Save the Internet (www.savetheinternet.com). Maintained by activists who support net neutrality, Save the Internet includes status reports on the issue as well as a blog where supporters can make their arguments for free and fair access to the phone lines and wireless networks that carry information over the Internet.

SearchEngineWatch.com (SEO) (www.searchenginewatch.com). Search EngineWatch.com chronicles trends in Internet searching and includes links that explain search engine optimization and the use of search in social networking sites. The website also includes a rating system for assessing the performance of Google, Bing, and other search engines.

VirtualSalt (www.virtualsalt.com). Maintained by Robert Harris, a former college English professor, VirtualSalt includes guidelines for students to follow while searching for information online. Harris has also provided a list of dozens of search engines, many of which specialize in specific types of information, such as medicine, religion, and the arts.

Index

Note: Boldface page numbers indicate illustrations.

Picture Credits

Cover: Thinkstock/Photodisc

Maury Aaseng: 24, 29

AP Images: 5, 9, 46, 51, 54, 59

© Anthony J. Causi/Icon SMI/Corbis: 38

© Macduff Everton/Corbis: 15

© Kim Kulish/Corbis: 21

NASA/Science Photo Library: 36

© Str/Reuters/Corbis: 64

Thinkstock/Goodshoot: 71

About the Author

Hal Marcovitz is a former newspaper reporter and columnist who has written more than 150 books for young readers. As a journalist, he was called on to provide stories for both print and online readers. He makes his home in Chalfont, Pennsylvania.